Railway Crimes Committed in Victorian Britain

Railway Crimes Committed in Victorian Britain

Authenticated crimes and offences committed on Britain's railways during the nineteenth century.

Malcolm Clegg

PEN & SWORD
TRANSPORT
AN IMPRINT OF PEN & SWORD BOOKS LTD.
YORKSHIRE – PHILADELPHIA

First published in Great Britain in 2023 by
Pen and Sword Transport
An imprint of
Pen & Sword Books Ltd.
Yorkshire - Philadelphia

ISBN 9781399085816

Typeset in INDIA By IMPEC eSolutions
Printed and bound in England by CPI Group (UK) Ltd, Croydon CR0 4YY.

Pen & Sword Books Ltd incorporates the imprints of Pen & Sword Books Archaeology,
Atlas, Aviation, Battleground, Discovery, Family History, History, Maritime, Military,
Naval, Politics, Railways, Select, Transport, True Crime, Fiction, Frontline Books,
Leo Cooper, Praetorian Press, Seaforth Publishing, Wharncliffe and White Owl.

For a complete list of Pen & Sword titles please contact

PEN & SWORD BOOKS LIMITED
47 Church Street, Barnsley, South Yorkshire, S70 2AS, England
E-mail: enquiries@pen-and-sword.co.uk
Website: www.pen-and-sword.co.uk

or

PEN AND SWORD BOOKS
1950 Lawrence Rd, Havertown, PA 19083, USA
E-mail: Uspen-and-sword@casematepublishers.com
Website: www.penandswordbooks.com

Front Cover
A Great Eastern Railway D14 Class 4-4-0 heads an express of mixed carriage stock
in 1910. (Stumpf, Scott-Morgan Archives)

Back Cover
A London South Western Railway, Drummond E10 Class 4-2-0 heads a south bound
express train through Clapham Cutting in 1912. (Stumpf, Scott-Morgan Archives)

Contents

Preface

Having served a thirty-year career with the British Transport Police, I have often been asked about the nature of crimes and types of offences which occur on the railways. Many people fail to realise that the majority of crimes and offences committed on the railways are generally the just the same as those committed elsewhere.

The main difference is that since the railways were first created almost 200 years ago, parliamentary legislation has created hundreds of additional offences, ranging from minor infringements to serious crimes for exclusive use on the railways. As well as dealing with and punishing transgressors, railway legislation has been designed to regulate the railways, ensure that trains are a safe mode of transport and afford protection to the millions of passengers being transported, as well as other members of the public and staff working the railway networks.

The Victorian era began in 1837, not long after the first railways were built and covered a period in history when vast changes were taking place in industrial development and railway technology. As the railways entered the twentieth century and the Victorian age became confined to the history books, the railways of Britain had been dramatically transformed from a rudimentary transport system into what many people would consider to be an essential modern-day railway network.

This book gives a factual account of the types of crime and offences committed on Britain's railways throughout those early years, by both members of the public and railway employees.

Malcolm Clegg
2023

Introduction

The first significant purpose-built railways anywhere in the world for carrying both freight and passengers are generally accepted as being the Stockton and Darlington Railway and the Liverpool and Manchester Railway which opened in 1825 and 1830 respectively. When Queen Victoria ascended to the throne in 1837, just 500 miles of railway track had been constructed in Britain, but this was just the start of a period in British history which later became known as the years of 'Railway Mania' when a frenzied scurry took place to build new railways as money poured in from speculators seeking to make their fortunes.

By 1845, 2,441 miles of railway had been constructed which increased to 6,000 miles over the next five years. In 1870, almost 425 million passengers and vast amounts of freight were being transported on 16,000 miles of railway operating nationwide. At the end of Victoria's reign in January 1901, a railway network consisting of well over 100 different railway companies was operating on 22,000 miles of track stretching the length and breadth of Britain. Throughout the nineteenth century, when class distinction was very pronounced, there were three different classes of travel (first, second and third) for passengers travelling on Britain's railways.

From the dawn of the first railways, it quickly became apparent that this new and revolutionary form of transport would have unwanted side effects, one of which was crime. Crime, especially the pilfering of goods from barges, had already been a problem on the canal networks of Britain before the advent of the railways and it was realised that a vast railway network would create a much bigger problem than anything ever experienced on the inland waterways.

The network of railways built during the nineteenth century was owned by private railway companies who were commercial organisations. Directors of these companies were aware that they had a duty and obligation to ensure the safety and protection of all passengers, staff and other members of the public using their premises. It was also their responsibility to provide adequate security within their own organisations. In order to achieve these aims, most railway companies employed large numbers of railway policemen who soon became a common sight in Victorian Britain.

Almost all types of crime which could be committed in the cities, towns and villages of Britain in the nineteenth century could also be committed on the railway. In addition, railway legislation created a multitude of additional crimes and criminal offences which were exclusive to the railways. In the main, specific railway offences were designed to protect and safeguard railway premises, property, members of staff and members of the public. Offences were also created in an attempt to ensure the uninterrupted smooth running of the railways.

Parliament also passed railway legislation which authorised railway policemen to forcibly eject people from the railway where necessary, as well as providing powers of arrest to assist them in administering law and order and enforcing legislation.

Some of the legal jargon used by the judiciary during the nineteenth century has since changed and is no longer in common usage. In order to assist readers, a few examples of such terminology are explained below.

Although used in Scotland for hundreds of years, the term 'theft' was seldom used in England and Wales during the nineteenth and early twentieth centuries. The legal and common word used to describe stealing was that of 'larceny'. There were various categories of larceny. A person who stole property would be guilty of 'simple larceny'. If a person stole property from his or her employer it was classified as 'larceny servant' which is mentioned quite frequently in this book, due to the fact that when railway staff stole items from the railway (their employer), they were guilty of that offence.

Larceny servant was considered by the judiciary to be more serious than simple larceny as the offender was abusing a position of trust by stealing property entrusted into his or her care. This was reflected in sentencing and offenders invariably received harsher sentences after being found guilty of 'larceny servant' than those convicted of 'simple larceny'. Other forms of larceny were by 'trick', 'intimidation', 'mistake' and 'finding'. Those examples do not appear in this particular book.

With the introduction of the 1968 Theft Act in England and Wales, the offence of larceny became obsolete in the statute books and was replaced by a new offence of theft which came into effect on 1 January 1969.

Another common offence in the nineteenth century was that of 'embezzlement' which also appears in this book. The offence of embezzlement was basically when an employee stole money from his or her employer by way of fraud. This was a specific offence under the former 'larceny acts' but was re-defined as a form of theft after the Larceny Act of 1916 was repealed by the Theft Act of 1968.

Some sentences imposed by the judiciary during the nineteenth century are seen by many people today as being harsh and sometimes barbaric. Whilst some terms such as whipping and flogging are self-explanatory, other terms may be less familiar.

The term 'penal servitude' was an extremely common form of punishment handed out by the judiciary during the nineteenth and early twentieth centuries. 'Penal servitude' meant imprisonment with hard labour.

When prisoners were sentenced to a term of imprisonment exceeding three months, they could be ordered to carry out forced hard labour in addition to being incarcerated. Hard labour was carried out at the beginning of a sentence for a specified designated period of time up to a maximum of three months, after which the remainder of the sentence would be completed in prison without the hard labour. Hard labour was first introduced as a sentence in Britain in 1776. The three month maximum time for hard labour was reduced to one month a century later in 1877. A person had to be sixteen or over in order to be sentenced to hard labour. Penal servitude continued to be a form of judicial punishment well into the twentieth century, until it was abolished in 1948, along with flogging.

Another type of sentence which was quite frequently imposed by the judiciary in the nineteenth century, was that of 'penal transportation' or transportation as it was commonly known.

All convicts sentenced to transportation from Britain during the nineteenth century, were sent to either Australia or Van Diemen's Land (modern-day Tasmania). The sentence of transportation was abolished in 1857, although prisoners already sentenced continued to be transported to penal colonies for a further decade until the last prison ship set sail for Western Australia in 1867. In the early eighteenth century, before penal colonies had been established in Australia and Tasmania, all convicts transported from Britain were sent to North America or the West Indies. These destinations ceased to be used after the American Revolution took place in 1776.

All the cases referred to in this book are factual accounts of criminal offences which either took place on the railways of England, Scotland and Wales during the Victorian era or were closely associated with and involved the railways. Almost all of the information has been obtained through many hours of research carried out by delving into nineteenth century newspaper archives.

Chapter 1

Targeting the Royal Mail

West Country Mail Trains Raided

On Monday 1 January 1849, the Great Western Railway Up mail train left Plymouth at 6.35pm bound for London. The train itself was part mail train and part passenger train, the formation of which was as follows; Front to back: locomotive and tender; travelling post office Coach (TPO), which was occupied by post office staff engaged in the sorting of mail; a post office tender (a locked van) where full mailbags were transferred from the TPO coach at various stations to be stored, after having been sorted by post office staff; a first-class passenger coach, followed by six second class coaches; and finally a guard's van at the rear of the train. After departing from Plymouth, the train called at intermediate stations to Exeter, before travelling on to Bridgwater, where it arrived on time at half past ten in the evening. Upon arrival at Bridgwater, numerous mail bags, which had been sorted, were removed from the TPO and placed in the post office tender which was then securely locked before the train departed for Bristol.

Shortly before midnight, the train arrived at Bristol and the guard went to the post office tender in order to take out the Bristol mail bags for delivery to Bristol Post Office. He unlocked the van and went inside. To his utter disbelief, he discovered that most of the mail inside had been tampered with. Seals on the bags had been broken and the strings cut. Letters and other contents of the bags were strewn over the floor of the van. The guard immediately informed two travelling post office officials who were inside the TPO accompanying the mail. They went inside the post office tender, made a very cursory examination of the contents and came to the conclusion that a considerable amount of money, registered items, and high value mail had been stolen. After the post office authorities at Bristol were notified, it was decided that the remaining contents of the post office tender should continue on to London, where arrangements would be made for the train to be met at Paddington Station by senior post office officials and a full check carried out.

The Great Western Railway police at Bristol together with the Bristol and Exeter Railway police started immediate enquiries and it was quickly established that when the train left Bridgwater Station, the post office tender was intact and the doors were locked. The train did not stop between Bridgwater and Bristol. It therefore appeared that the pilfering had somehow taken place whilst the train was in motion between the two stations. The door locks did not appear to have been tampered with, so it was assumed that someone on the train had left a compartment and made their way along the outside running board of the train to the mail tender and unlocked the door with a railway carriage key which was issued to railway staff. The thief or thieves, after opening the mail bags, could either have jumped from the moving train or made their way back to the compartment from whence they came. The inside of the post office tender was well lit by an oil lamp hanging from the roof, in the centre of the vehicle.

Whilst enquiries were continuing in the West Country, Colonel Maberly, Secretary of the Post Office in London and officer in charge of the post office investigation branch, together with Mr Peacock, a senior solicitor in the post office legal department, had taken charge of the Post Office side of the investigation, making it a priority in establishing the true extent and value of the stolen property. Later that afternoon, however, they received some very unwelcome news.

It transpired that the previous evening (the same day that the raid on the mail train took place), the Down mail train departed Paddington at 8.55pm, and arrived at Bristol at 1.15am the following morning. All the mail bags on the train were intact when the train arrived at Bristol. The train left Bristol and travelled non-stop to Bridgwater. Upon arrival, when the post office tender was unlocked it was found that most of the mail bags had been cut open and interfered with, in an identical manner to that of the previous incident. It seemed obvious from the methods used that the persons who had interfered with the mail bags on the Up mail train between Bridgwater and Bristol, were the same culprits who had then travelled back to Bridgwater just over an hour later on the Down mail train and committed an almost identical crime on the return journey. Police were now investigating the two matters.

At the time that Colonel Maberly and Mr Peacock received the news of the second incident, they were unaware that some startling new developments had taken place in the West Country. When the second incident was discovered at Bridgwater, the matter was again immediately reported to the post office officials in the Travelling Post Office coach. As luck would have it, the two postal officials in the coach to whom it was reported were the same officials to whom the first incident had been reported on the Up mail train at Bristol. The two officials had completed the first part of their tour of duty at Bristol on the Up mail train before changing trains at Bristol to work the Down mail train back to Plymouth. Having had time to reflect on the method used in the first incident, the clerks realised that the persons responsible for this second incident were in all probability still on the train. Station staff and the train crew were warned to be vigilant.

One of the passengers on the down mail train that night happened to be Mr Barlow, who was one of the directors of the Great Western Railway Company. As a result of the mail theft being discovered at Bridgwater, the train was held longer than normal. Barlow enquired of the guard the reason for the delay and he was informed of what had happened. Barlow then took it upon himself to take charge of the situation. He spoke to post office staff and was informed that the culprits were possibly still on the train and likely to be in the first-class coach which was attached to the post office tender. Mr Barlow instructed the guard to examine the tickets of passengers in that coach to ascertain their destination.

It was established that there were two men in the first-class compartment next to the post office tender. Both men had first class tickets to Exeter. The next adjoining compartment had one occupant, a male passenger travelling to Modbury in Devon.

Barlow then went to the first compartment and spoke to the two occupants. They were sitting in opposite ends of the compartment. He told them what had happened and asked if they had seen anything suspicious. Both men stated that they were travelling alone and did not know each other. They further stated that they had no knowledge of the incident and had not seen or heard anything. Barlow then went to the next compartment and spoke to the occupant, Mr Andrews, who was a solicitor from Modbury. Andrews had not seen or heard anything untoward, but he was able to tell Barlow that the two men in the next compartment joined the train at Bristol. They appeared to be travelling together and after entering the compartment, one of the men pulled down the blinds on the compartment windows.

As a result, Barlow's suspicions were aroused, and he decided to travel with the two men in the first compartment to prevent them communicating with each other. The train then continued to Taunton which was the next stop. Upon arrival at Taunton, Mr Clark, the night station superintendent, went to the compartment, accompanied by Joseph Gibbons, an off-duty police superintendent from Plymouth who just happened to be a passenger on the train. Superintendent Gibbons spoke to the men who once again denied all knowledge of the incident and again denied knowing each other. He asked the men for their names and addresses. One of the men gave his particulars as Henry Poole of New North Road, Exeter. He was about thirty years of age. The other man refused to give his name and address. Superintendent Gibbons searched the two men and found them both to be in possession of a watch, and some cash. In addition, Poole was found to be in possession of some pieces of string, similar to the type used for securing mail bags and some sealing wax, of the type used to seal mailbags.

Clark in the meantime made a search of the compartment and, pushed into a corner beneath the seat occupied by Poole, he found fourteen small parcels and packages with postal stamps, all bearing addresses in the West of England. Wrapped in a handkerchief he found three diamond rings, three gold rings and a watch case. Also, beneath the seat was a black cap and two crepe face masks. Poole stated that the items were nothing to do with him, he had never seen them before and they must have been in the compartment when he boarded the train at Bristol. Superintendent Gibbons remained with the men until the train arrived at Exeter, where he handed the men and the recovered property over to police. The two men were taken into custody.

The identity of Henry Poole was later confirmed and it was established that he was a former train guard employed by the Great Western Railway Company who had been dismissed from the service some nine months earlier for misconduct. He was believed to have been involved in stealing a number of gold sovereigns which were stolen from a train whilst in transit. Poole was working as a guard on the train in question and had access to them, but he denied stealing them and was never prosecuted due to lack of evidence. During his employment on the railway, he would have been issued with a railway carriage key of the type used to lock and unlock carriage doors, including ones fitted to the travelling post office coach and tender. It was quite possible that he did not hand the key back to the railway authorities when his services were dispensed with, and he used it to enter the post office tender on the mail train.

Both men continued to deny all knowledge of both incidents, but there was little doubt that they were responsible. It was assumed that either Poole on his own, or both men left the railway compartments on both trains and entered the adjoining post office tender vans by way of the running board. Having unlocked the tender door with the carriage key which Poole had been issued with whilst working as a guard, it would then have been relatively simple to cut open and rifle the mail bags before returning to the passenger compartment. Poole could have disposed of the carriage key at any time before being searched by Superintendent Gibbons. The running time of the train between Bridgwater and Bristol (and vice versa) was approximately one hour and ten minutes, which gave the men ample time to commit the crimes. It was also thought that Poole intended to tie and re-seal the mail bags which they had pilfered, using the string and sealing wax found in his possession when he was arrested, but for some reason he had not done so.

Enquires in Bristol later revealed that two men matching the descriptions of the suspects had been seen in the Talbot Inn in the city shortly after midnight on the day in question. They remained in the public house for about one hour and left in time to return to the station and catch the Down mail train back to Exeter. No property stolen from the Up mail train was ever recovered, and it is thought that it may have been secreted or handed to an accomplice in Bristol.

The two men were charged on two counts that they, on 2 January 1849, in the county of Somerset, did steal twelve postal letters, three diamond rings valued at £70, three gold rings valued at £70, one watch case valued at £2 and other items (total of £18,000 in today's money), the property of the Postmaster General.

Both men appeared before Magistrates at Exeter Guildhall Court on Saturday, 20 January 1849. They pleaded not guilty. The second man still refused to divulge any details about himself, including his name and address. Both men were remanded in custody to stand trial at the next Devon Assizes.

The two men appeared before Lord Denman at the Devon Assize Court in Exeter on Friday, 23 March 1849. The prosecution was conducted by Mr Rogers and Mr Poulden. Henry Poole was represented by Mr Cockburn and Mr Slade and the other defendant, who now gave his name as Edward Nightingale from London, was represented by Mr Ball and Mr Stone.

The case was put before the jury who, after hearing the evidence, deliberated for approximately forty-five minutes before returning a verdict of guilty on both counts against each of the defendants. Lord Denman stated that there was no doubt whatsoever that the jury had returned the correct verdict. He sentenced both men to fifteen years transportation. After hearing the verdict, Poole fainted and had to be carried from the courtroom.

Henry Poole and Edward Nightingale both denied all knowledge of these crimes before, throughout and after the proceedings. No charges were ever brought against them in relation to the first raid on the post office mails between Bridgwater and Bristol on Monday, 1 January 1849, due to lack of evidence and no stolen property being found. The charges which they faced related to offences committed on the 2 January 1849, which were based almost entirely on circumstantial, albeit significant, evidence, which included the fact that fourteen small packages of stolen property were recovered from under the seat in the compartment in which they were travelling. The post office never made public the nature or value of the property stolen, but it was estimated by some newspapers at the time, that the property stolen was valued in excess of £200,000 which in today's money would in excess of £26 million. That of course, in the true tradition of newspaper reporting, may have been something of an exaggeration.

In an ironic twist to this case, George Nightingale, from Holloway, North London, who was the father of the defendant Edward Nightingale, had been arrested some twelve years earlier in May 1827. He was held in Newgate Prison, London after being charged with robbing the Royal Mail which was (prior to the building of a railway) being transported by road from the port of Dover to London. He was accused of stealing a foreign (Italian) mailbag but was acquitted due to lack of evidence, after a notice of alibi was given, which showed that at the time of the robbery, he was visiting the West of England of all places.

Former Railway Porter Steals Mailbag in an Act of Revenge

On Wednesday 12 September 1888, Herbert James Leadbeater, aged 21, a former porter employed by the London and North Western Railway Company at Morley Station in the West Riding of Yorkshire, boarded a Leeds train at Batley station. He sat in an empty second-class compartment at the rear of the train, next to the guard's van. The train departed from Batley and stopped at Morley station a few minutes later. The train guard alighted from the guard's van and walked along the platform towards the front of the train. Upon seeing this, Leadbeater opened his compartment door on the non-platform side of the train and jumped onto the track. He walked back a few yards, opened the guard's van door (non-platform side), removed a high value mailbag from the guard's van, closed the door and took the mailbag back to his compartment. The mailbag had been placed in the guard's van at Batley and was destined for Leeds. The train guard returned to his guard's van, unaware that the mailbag had been stolen and the train continued its journey towards Leeds. As the train approached Churwell, which was the next station, Leadbeater threw the mailbag out of the compartment window onto a railway embankment. He alighted from the train at Churwell, walked back along the side of the railway line and retrieved the mailbag. He then took the bag to his father's home in Batley. In the meantime, the train had arrived at its destination in Leeds where the mailbag and contents were found to be missing.

Enquiries into the missing mail bag were carried out by Detective Chief Inspector Richards of the London and North Western Railway Police, stationed at Manchester and on Friday, 20 September 1888, together with Detective Howells and Mr Kirby from the Post Office, DCI Richards visited Leadbeater's home in Morley and carried out a search of the premises.

During the search, they recovered a number of securities, cheques and postal orders to the value of £6,800 and two watches, each valued at £10 (totalling almost £931,000 in today's money) from beneath his bed. Leadbeater admitted stealing the mail bag, saying he was sorry. When asked about the large number of letters which had been in the bag, he stated that they were just letters, of no use to him so he had burned them. He then took the officers to a field about a mile from his home where they recovered the remains of the empty mailbag and some debris which were the remains of the letters which he had burned. Leadbeater also admitted having already cashed some of the stolen postal orders.

Herbert James Leadbeater was arrested and later charged. He appeared before Dewsbury Magistrates Court on the 28 September 1888 and was committed to Leeds Assizes to stand trial on a charge of stealing the mailbag and contents.

He appeared before Baron Pollock at the West Riding of Yorkshire Autumn Assizes at Leeds Town Hall on Saturday 15 December 1888. He pleaded guilty to stealing the mailbag. The court heard that the defendant was employed as a porter at Morley station until he had his foot amputated in an accident whilst working on the railway. He was given the sum of £60 in compensation (£8,000 in today's money) and his services were dispensed with due to him being physically unfit to perform his duties as a direct result of the injury. The court also heard that this crime was premeditated, as Leadbeater confessed that he had planned the mailbag theft as an act of revenge against the London and North Western Railway Company who he blamed for his accident, although he told the court that he subsequently regretted his actions. Leadbeater was sentenced to eighteen months penal servitude.

Railway Employee Stole High Value Mail

On Tuesday, 5 December 1893, a passenger train departed from Liverpool Street Station in London at five o'clock in the afternoon and travelled non-stop to Ipswich on the Great Eastern Railway. Attached to the rear of the train were three post office mail vans, containing parcels and mail bags being sent from Mount Pleasant sorting office in London to East Anglia. One van contained mail for Ipswich, another contained mail for Lowestoft and the third was carrying mail for Yarmouth. This was a daily occurrence. After the contents of the three vans had been loaded at Liverpool Street, the vans were locked. Upon arrival of the train at Ipswich, the Ipswich van was detached from the train and later unloaded in order for the contents to be transferred to the local postal sorting office for distribution. At 6.46pm, the train left Ipswich and continued to Beccles where it was divided to form two separate trains, one destined for Lowestoft and the other for Yarmouth. The two post office vans were each attached to the appropriate trains for their destinations.

The Lowestoft train arrived at its destination on time and the mail was transferred to Lowestoft Post Office where it was checked and found to be intact. The Yarmouth train arrived at its destination and the mail was off loaded and transferred to the Yarmouth Post Office for sorting. One of the mail bags which contained mainly loose letters, was also the mail bag which contained high value mail. This bag was a standard type mailbag, tied with string which was threaded through loop holes at intervals around the top of the bag, pulled tight before being labelled and sealed with sealing wax. A symbol which randomly appeared amongst other symbols on the label of the bag, identified the bag as containing the high value mail. The high value items were inside a small sealed bag which was loose amongst the rest of the bag contents. Consequently, the mail bag with the high value mail was separated from all the other bags upon arrival to be opened by a senior postal inspector.

Before even opening the outer bag, an eagle-eyed inspector immediately realised that the mail bag had been tampered with. The original string had been cut and the bag tied with a new piece of string. The original seal however had been left intact. The new string was genuine post office string, as used in County Post Offices, but it differed from that used in the main London sorting office at Mount Pleasant, who used string made from hemp. Upon opening the mailbag, the inspector discovered the letters intact, but the high value bag was missing.

It was later confirmed by the London sorting office that when the mailbag was dispatched, it contained 240 letters, a quantity of sundry circulars and some newspapers. In addition, it also contained the sealed high value bag which in turn contained three registered letters. One of the registered letters was sent by Messrs Glyn Mills and Co. of London to Alcon and Youell's Bank and contained £125 in cash, made up of twenty-three £5 notes and one £10 note (total £17,000 in today's money). It was later established that William Harry Lewis, cashier to Messrs Glyn Mills and Co. had kept the serial numbers of all the bank notes which he had dispatched to Youell's bank.

Upon discovering that the high value bag had been stolen, two senior post office officials liaised with Inspector Power of the Great Eastern Railway Police at Ipswich and enquires commenced. Inspector Power arranged for detective officers to visit various banks and shops in Ipswich, where they recovered three of the stolen five-pound notes which had already been exchanged.

At the time, old white five-pound notes had to be endorsed with a signature of the person exchanging them and each of the three notes recovered were all endorsed and signed in the name of Burgess. The serial numbers confirmed that the notes were stolen from the mail train.

Inspector Power later obtained a book from the railway staff office which contained signatures of all the railway employees working at Ipswich station. A close examination of the book revealed the handwritten signature of a railway porter by the name of Percival Joseph Buddery, appeared similar to the endorsements on the three five-pound notes.

Further enquiries revealed that the Ipswich Station Master, Mr Fitzjohn, saw Buddery standing on the station platform when the train arrived from London some time after half past six on 5 December. Fitzjohn further stated that he did not see Buddery after the train departed at 6.46pm. Buddery had signed off duty at 6.50pm in the duty book, although it was conceded that he could have made the entry a few minutes earlier. The 6.46pm departure was the last train to Yarmouth that day. Fitzjohn confirmed that Buddery did not have permission to travel to Yarmouth on that train. Enquiries at Yarmouth confirmed that Buddery was seen on Yarmouth station early the following morning, waiting to catch the first train back to Ipswich.

Inspector Power was therefore of the firm opinion that Buddery used his railway carriage key to enter the post office van at Ipswich, then travelled inside the van to Yarmouth. He opened the mail bag during the journey and removed the high value bag before re-tying the mail bag. Buddery would then have been able to alight at Yarmouth before staff arrived to unload the post office van and remain in Yarmouth overnight before returning to Ipswich by the first available train the following morning.

Buddery was subsequently arrested on suspicion of stealing the high value mail bag and interviewed by Inspector Power who informed him of the enquiry he was making. Inspector Power informed Buddery that one of the missing letters had contained £125 in bank notes, three of which had been recovered after being cashed in Ipswich by a person matching his description. Buddery denied being the person concerned. Inspector Power produced the bank notes and pointed to the name Burgess written on each of the notes, stating that in his opinion, the handwriting belonged to him. Buddery denied that the handwriting was his but agreed to take part in an identification parade.

Some time later, Buddery lined up with six other men of a similar age and description. A shop proprietor, Mr Croydon, entered the room and immediately identified Buddery as the person who tendered the five-pound note in his shop. Shop owner Mrs Dance then entered the room and also picked out Buddery as being the person who entered her premises and endorsed the note in the name of Burgess in order the exchange it. Buddery was later charged with stealing a mail bag belonging to the Post Office.

On Thursday, 23 December 1893, Percival Joseph Buddery, a porter, aged 23, employed by the Great Eastern Railway Company, of 4, Pleasant Terrace, Ranelagh Road, Ipswich appeared before Ipswich Magistrates Court charged with stealing a post letter bag and contents belonging to the post office. Mr E.P. Ridley appeared on behalf of the prosecution and Mr H. Chamberlain represented the defendant. Buddery pleaded 'not guilty' to the charge and evidence was put before the magistrates. After considering the evidence, the magistrates committed Buddery to stand trial at the next Assize Court. There was no application for bail, and he was remanded in custody.

Buddery appeared before Mr Justice Cave at the Suffolk Winter Assizes which were held in Ipswich on 18 January 1894. Mr Philbrick QC and Mr Bullock appeared on behalf of the prosecution. Mr Simon Reeve represented Buddery.

The accused now pleaded guilty to the charge and Mr R.R. Martins, the Mayor of Great Yarmouth, was called to speak of the early good character of the prisoner. The judge, taking this into consideration, sentenced Buddery to twelve months penal servitude.

Chapter 2

Stealing From the Railway

Silver Bullion Vanishes

Goods in transit on the railways have always been an easy target for thieves and whilst the majority of goods stolen in this fashion are unattended goods, removed from railway wagons and vans stabled in railway sidings or goods yards, or taken from goods depots and railway stations, some items were stolen after having left the railway premises altogether for delivery to their final destination by road.

One such incident occurred towards the end of the Victorian era when an extremely valuable consignment of silver bullion being transported by the Midland Railway Company suddenly vanished from the streets of London whilst on the last leg if its journey by road to its final destination in the heart of the city.

On Tuesday, 24 September 1895, five wooden cases containing a total of thirty-one silver ingots were sent from Messrs Vivian and Co. Swansea to Messrs Sharp and Williams of Great Winchester Street, London EC. This was a regular consignment which was sent by railway, twice weekly on Tuesdays and Thursdays. The consignment was despatched from Swansea on the Great Western Railway and travelled by way of Cardiff, Newport and Hereford, to the Great Western Railway Company and the Midland Railway Company joint railway station at Worcester Shrub Hill. There the consignment was transferred onto the Midland Railway for the final leg of its journey by train to the Midland Railway Goods Depot at St Pancras in London. The wagon containing the solid silver ingots arrived safely at St Pancras goods depot shortly before seven o'clock the following morning, Wednesday, 25 September.

The five cases which contained the ingots were made of strong timber secured with screws and bolts and bound with iron bands. The ingots themselves were just over 15in long (38cm) x 5in wide (12.7cm) x 4in deep

(10.16cm). Each ingot was stamped with the initials V and S, together with a serial number, consecutively upwards from 556. They varied in weight from 947 ounces (26.8kg) to 1,271 ounces (36kg), the total weight being 34,984 ounces (991.7kg). They were all pure solid silver. After the consignment was unloaded from the railway wagon it was transferred to a Midland Railway horse-drawn delivery van number 968 which was painted in the Midland Railway Company livery of red and blue. The van was securely locked. The carter and his boy delivery assistant left the depot shortly afterwards to deliver the silver bullion to its destination.

After leaving the goods depot, the carter drove his vehicle a short distance where he pulled up outside a coffee house near Phoenix Street and Ossulston Street. The carter and the boy went into the coffee house for breakfast, leaving the horse and van unattended outside. When they returned some twenty or thirty minutes later, the carter to his utter amazement and disbelief found that his horse and the van had disappeared. The boy assistant ran back to the Midland (St Pancras) Station, followed by the carter, where the matter was reported to the Midland Railway Police. The Metropolitan Police were informed and circulated the description of a chestnut horse and a Midland Railway delivery van bearing the number 968.

Within one hour, the horse and the van were found abandoned in Spencer Street approximately one mile from where they had been taken. The iron bands around the five packing cases had been broken off and the fastenings unbolted. It came as little surprise to find that all the silver ingots had been stolen. The total value of the stolen ingots was £4,900 (approximately £677,000 in today's money).

Superintendent Capp of the Midland Railway Police travelled from Derby to London where he liaised with Detective Inspector White and Detective Sergeant Masey, of the Midland Railway Police at St Pancras. Details were circulated to all silversmiths and jewellers within the metropolis to be on the lookout for any of the stolen ingots. The driver of the delivery van was quizzed at great length but was not thought to have been involved. He had been working for the railway company for a number of years.

Superintendent Capp and his officers slowly began to glean information about the crime. A clerk by the name of Parker came forward and volunteered information that he had seen the horse and van being driven along Phoenix Street on the day in question, followed by a man whom he knew as Henry Bailey, who jumped onto the tailboard of the van. Bailey was subsequently arrested at his home in Kentish Town and four silver ingots were recovered from beneath his bed. He was subsequently charged with stealing the horse and van containing the ingots. He pleaded not guilty at a subsequent court appearance but was convicted and sentenced to three and a half years penal servitude, followed by three years police supervision.

Alexander Sarti, the manager of Messrs Elkington's, silversmiths and electroplating works, Myddleton Street, Clerkenwell, was arrested at his place of work. Two of the stolen silver ingots were found in a stripping bath within the works, having been placed there with the obvious intention of removing identification marks. He was also sentenced to three-and-a-half year's penal servitude after being convicted of receiving the ingots, knowing them to have been stolen. Sadly, Mr Sarti committed suicide by taking carbolic acid at his home shortly after being released from prison.

As enquiries progressed, another ingot was recovered after being found abandoned in school grounds at Camden Town. An unsuccessful attempt to saw it with a hacksaw had been made. A further four of the stolen ingots were recovered by Chief Inspector Palmer of the Midland Railway Police from an address in Graham Road, Dalston, Hackney, whilst officers from the Metropolitan Police dug up a further six which had been buried in the back garden of the house. Other ingots which were recovered led to two other men being arrested. George Barrett from Devon Road, Bow, was sentenced to five years penal servitude, and Edward Gray, also from Bow, received eighteen months hard labour. A determined investigation carried out in this case, jointly by the Midland Railway Police and the Metropolitan Police, had achieved considerable success and out of the thirty-one ingots of silver which were stolen, a total of twenty-seven were recovered.

Stealing Coal

Stealing coal from the railways was an extremely common offence during the nineteenth and twentieth centuries and there was an abundance of coal to steal. To illustrate the enormity of the problem, in the month of June 1897, over seventy individuals appeared before Alderman Sanders a Cardiff Magistrate, after being charged with stealing coal from railway wagons on the Taff Vale railway at one single location in Cardiff. Similar problems were occurring at hundreds of other locations, nationwide.

The industrial revolution was fuelled by coal which was also used for cooking and heating by almost every household in the land. Millions of tons of coal could be seen all over the railway network, piled into open wagons which were often unattended in sidings, coal yards and depots. Coal could be found stacked in heaps or just lying along the ground seemingly everywhere. Many coal merchants had their premises on railway property, in order to access it quickly as it arrived by coal trains from nearby collieries. During the nineteenth century, coal merchants delivered coal locally using horse and carts but as the twentieth century progressed, motor lorries were introduced to replace horses and carts which were virtually obsolete by the end of the 1950s.

Although vast amounts of coal were stolen from the railway on a daily basis, it was generally stolen in small quantities for local household consumption, often by the poor who could ill afford to buy it, or as a means of saving them money, as anyone attempting to sell stolen coal in large quantities would quickly attract attention to themselves, unless of course they themselves were coal merchants which did happen on occasions. Some quite severe punishments were imposed by the courts, particularly during the nineteenth century for what many people today would consider to be rather petty crimes. Juveniles convicted of stealing coal (of which there were many), were dealt with alongside adults, as juvenile courts were not introduced into Britain until the twentieth century.

Boys Stole Coal from Railway Sidings

On 17 September 1887, five boys appeared before magistrates in South Wales where they pleaded guilty to stealing a small quantity of coal from some railway sidings in the lower station yard at Tenby on the Pembroke and Tenby Railway.

Alfred Davies, aged 15, was sent to prison for ten days and afterwards, detained for three years in a reformatory, Robert Jones, aged 9, ordered to serve three years in an industrial school, Thomas Gibbs, aged 8, George Johnson, aged 10 and Joseph Upham, aged 11, were each fined 6d and ordered to pay costs.

Signalman Caught Stealing Coal

On Tuesday, 16 February 1869, John Lewis, a railway signalman employed by the Monmouthshire Railway and Canal Company, was caught stealing coal from a railway wagon. He was later sentenced to two months imprisonment with hard labour and dismissed from his employment with the railway company.

Provost Declares Coal Thefts Becoming Far Too Common

On 18 October 1897, the *Edinburgh Evening News* reported that two women were fined for stealing coal from railway wagons opposite West Lothian pottery, when they appeared before Bo'ness Police Court. The Provost (Scottish Magistrate) told the court that this type of offence was becoming far too common and needed to be stopped.

Hidden Dangers of Stealing Coal from The Railway

On 20 May 1891, Mrs Helena Stamburgh appeared before Newport Magistrates Court, charged with stealing coal from the Dock Street Sidings of the Great Western Railway on 20 April that year. The court heard that Mrs Stamburgh was picking up coal which had fallen from the top of coal wagons, when she was caught between the buffers of two wagons which had been put in motion by shunting operations. As a result, she suffered two broken ribs, a crushed arm and had been laid up for one month under the care of a doctor. She pleaded guilty to stealing coal but told the court that she could not afford to buy it, her husband was out of work at the time and because of her injuries, she considered that she had already suffered enough. The court agreed that she had suffered as a result of injuries sustained and after reiterating the dangers of going onto the railway, sentenced her to just one day imprisonment.

Youths Suffer Harsh Sentences

On 21 June 1866, five boys named as William Hall aged 16, Daniel Hickson aged 16, William McLaren aged 13, James Dallas aged 15 and William Cook aged 14, all from Greenock in Scotland, appeared before Greenock Police Court, charged with stealing coal from a truck in some railway sidings on the Caledonian Railway.

Hall and Hickson pleaded not guilty to the charge against them, whilst the other three boys pleaded guilty. All five were found guilty and before passing sentence, the bailie (Scottish Magistrate) stated that the stealing of coals from the railway was 'getting so frequent by boys appearing before this court that an example must be made of the boys before me'. He sentenced Hall to twenty days' imprisonment, Hickson to fifteen days and the other three on account of their youth, to thirty lashes with a leather tawse (whip), or if not able to stand that, ten days imprisonment.

Children Stealing Coal

It was not just adults and boys who were responsible for stealing coal from the railway during the Victorian era. Young girls were also apprehended and taken before the courts as demonstrated when a 12-year-old appeared in court at Birkenhead in 1862.

On Friday, 24 October 1862, Mary Ann Willis, a 12-year-old girl, was seen by a police constable standing on a railway coal wagon at Birkenhead. She dragged one bag of coal weighing approximately one hundredweight (50kg) from the top of the wagon and let it fall to the ground. She climbed down from the wagon and dragged the bag of coal from the railway. As the constable approached the girl, her father appeared. He told the officer that he was at a loss to understand her behaviour. The girl was arrested and remanded in custody over the weekend. She appeared in court at Birkenhead the following Monday charged with stealing the bag of coal from the railway. The sympathetic magistrate informed her that he was taking a lenient view of the incident. He dismissed the charge against her and told her that he hoped that the three days which she had already spent in prison would be a salutary lesson to her.

Not all magistrates believed in a lenient approach towards children of tender years and some even considered the short sharp shock of corporal punishment to be the answer, as a young boy was to become all too painfully aware after his brush with the law in Buckinghamshire in 1872.

On 9 August 1872, Joseph Cleaver, just 9 years old, was caught stealing a small quantity of coal from a railway wagon belonging to the Newport Pagnell Railway Company. He appeared in court a week later where he was sentenced to be flogged with eight strokes of the rod and imprisoned for one day to teach him a lesson. The sentence was later carried out.

Other Items Stolen from The Railway

Boy Stole Oranges

On Monday, 12 December 1864, Henry Smith, a 13-year-old, appeared before Bristol Police Court for stealing oranges from a box at the Great Western Railway Station. He was sent to prison for seven days.

Staff Dismissed for Stealing Beer

Many railway employees have succumbed to stealing from their employer because it was often so easy to do so without being caught. Most individuals steal items for personal gain, or to sell for profit, although that is not always the case as two railway porters demonstrated when they came across something which they found very appealing to their taste.

In the spring of 1875, the Great Western Railway was experiencing repeated losses of beer from barrels which were inside railway vans at Bourne End Railway Station in Buckinghamshire. As a result, detectives arranged to keep observations at the station. On Thursday, 13 May 1875, detectives from the Great Western Railway Police saw two railway porters enter one of the vans containing barrels of beer and close the door behind them. The men remained in the van for some considerable time before they eventually staggered out, with one of them carrying a large canister. The detectives stopped them and found that the canister was full of beer. The porters themselves were quite inebriated. The officers went inside the van and found that a quantity of beer had been spilled from one of the barrels onto the floor of the van. When questioned, the porters said that they were just sampling the beer to ensure that it hadn't gone off. The porters appeared before High Wycombe Magistrates the following morning and after pleading guilty to stealing beer were each sentenced to three months imprisonment. Their happy days came to an end when they were both instantly dismissed from the employ of the Great Western Railway. The beer losses from Bourne End Railway Station came to an abrupt halt, which no doubt resulted in the railway detectives themselves celebrating their success.

Station Staff Plunder Goods

During the years of 1869 and 1870, regular complaints were received by Inspector Crawley of the Great Eastern Railway Police that items of goods in transit on the railway were being stolen whilst passing through Ipswich railway station. Extensive enquiries were made by detectives and a number of railway employees were arrested for stealing property belonging to the Great Eastern Railway Company. They all pleaded guilty when they appeared before the courts and received various terms of imprisonment as well as being dismissed from the services of the company.

One of the persons involved and amongst one of the last to be arrested was George Dale, age 38, who had been employed as a porter at Ipswich Station for fifteen years. He was arrested on 4 June 1870 and a search was made of his house. A considerable amount of property was recovered by police, which they believed had been stolen from the railway. The items included two Dutch cheeses, an opera cloak, a carpet, a travel bag containing a large number of personal items believed to have been stolen from railway passenger's luggage. Dale was subsequently charged with three specimen counts of larceny and he subsequently appeared before the Ipswich Borough Midsummer Quarter Sessions in July 1870. He admitted the offences and pleaded guilty to each of the three charges.

In passing sentence, the Recorder, William James Metcalf, said:

> You have pleaded guilty to stealing articles whilst you were a servant of the Railway Company. Other property also found at your house was undoubtedly the proceeds of crime. It is well known that there has been a great deal of plunder occurring on the Great Eastern Railway for a considerable time and a short time ago, a number of other prosecutions were made. It was hoped that those had put a stop to it. The sentences passed then, although to some extent heavy, were intended as a warning to other offenders. Several offenders on that occasion were brought here and it was hoped that the whole thing had been stamped out. You have been 15 years in the service of the company and you have been liberally paid the sum of 24s per week [£150 per week today] with the opportunities of receiving gratuities from passengers.

In sentencing Dale to five years penal servitude, the judge told him that due to the circumstances, it was the lowest term of imprisonment he was able to impose. Dale was then escorted from the dock to serve his sentence.

The Great Gold Dust Robbery

The SS *Great Western* was an oak-hulled paddle steamer, purpose-built for crossing the Atlantic Ocean from Bristol and Liverpool to New York. The vessel, which weighed 2,300 tons, was designed by Isambard Kingdom Brunel and built by William Patterson in Bristol in 1836 for the Great Western Steamship Company. During the next nine years, the ship made forty-five round trips across the Atlantic, before being sold to the Royal Mail Steam Packet Company in 1847, for operation on the West Indies run by the West India Royal Mail Company.

On Wednesday, 7 May 1851, the SS *Great Western* arrived at Southampton Docks with general cargo from America and the West Indies. Amongst this cargo was a vast quantity of gold which had been loaded onto the vessel in Panama. This gold shipment (principally gold dust) was extracted during the 1849/50 California gold rush and was being transported from California to the Bank of England in London.

The gold dust was contained inside tin canisters, which in turn were enclosed in wooden boxes which measured approximately 18in (4.72cm) in length, x 8in (20.32cm) wide, x 6in (15.24cm) deep. Each box weighed between 40 and 60lb (18-27kg). The exact number of boxes in the consignment is not known, but it was thought to be in excess of 200, in any event, a significant number. The total value of the consignment was estimated at the time to be in the region of £220,000 which in today's money would be worth a staggering £30 million.

During the afternoon of Thursday, 8 May 1851, the shipment of gold was unloaded from the SS *Great Western* and placed inside a covered transit shed, under the watchful eye of two customs officials, the packing superintendent and two shipping clerks, Mr Beer and Mr Beardmore from the West India Company's offices. Also present were two porter/messengers from the shipping company, Mr Winchip and Mr Quirk, who were there to assist Mr Beer and Mr Beardmore as necessary. Inside the transit shed, the consignment was loaded into four railway wagons. Forty-six boxes were loaded into wagon number 315 and the remaining boxes were loaded into the other three wagons. The details of every single box were meticulously checked by a tallyman and overseen by the superintendent and the shipping clerks. After the loading was complete, the railway wagons were sheeted with tarpaulin sheets which were securely tied to the wagons.

Coupled to the four wagons was a first class passenger coach which was intended for the exclusive use of Mr Beer, Mr Beardmore and the two porters who had been designated to accompany the consignment of gold to its destination at the Bank of England in London. The four wagons, together with the coach containing Beer, Beardmore and the porters, were shunted from the transit shed, off the docks where they were incorporated into the formation of a goods train destined for Nine Elms in London. There, the wagons would be unloaded, and the contents transferred to horse drawn wagons, for the final leg of the journey by road to the Bank of England.

The goods train was due to depart Southampton at 8pm that evening. The train itself was extremely long, which necessitated two steam locomotives being allocated to haul it. However, due to the late running of a preceding passenger train which was delayed whilst awaiting the arrival of a passenger ship, the goods train departed Southampton one hour late, at 9pm. It was the duty of the four men to keep an eye on the wagons containing the gold shipment at all times whilst the train was in transit and to alight at each station where the train stopped, to check that no persons were lurking near, or interfering with the wagons. There was a number of railway stations between Southampton and Nine Elms where the train was scheduled to stop to load and unload goods. The first stop was Bishopstoke, approximately six miles from Southampton. It was reported at the time that whilst the train was at Bishopstoke, Mr Beer and Mr Beardmore requested that the guard of the train get them some refreshments (alcoholic drinks) for their journey. It has been suggested that this practice took place at other stations along the line but was denied by the two men. The guard also admitted having taken refreshments himself, which included alcohol, whilst at Basingstoke station but it was confirmed by staff at Nine Elms that neither he, nor the two clerks were drunk when the train arrived at its destination.

The train arrived at Nine Elms Goods Depot at about 3am on Friday morning. It was met by Mr Thorne, the night duty goods traffic superintendent and members of his staff who immediately commenced unloading the contents of the goods train.

It was sometime between 5am and 6am that morning that an unwelcome discovery was made. Whilst unloading wagon number 315, it was noticed that the wagon only contained forty-three boxes of gold instead of the forty-six which were recorded on the consignment sheets. Repeated checks confirmed that three boxes were missing from the consignment. The missing boxes were marked as follows; the first box had a letter 'B' on the top and the initials 'N.M.R.' on the bottom. It weighed 53lb (24kg). The second box had the initials 'C.M.' on the top, and 'M.M.R.' on the bottom and it weighed 39lb 12oz (18kg). The third box had no weight mark but had the name 'D. Dunbar & Son' written on it. The total value of the three missing boxes was estimated at being £4,900 (over £670,000 today).

Upon discovery of the theft, the local Metropolitan police were summoned and Sergeant Eastman of 'V' division attended, together with Thomas Bent, a Detective Constable in the Metropolitan Police who was attached solely to the South Western Railway Company. Details of the crime were circulated by telegraph to Southampton and all intermediate railway stations. Details were circulated to both the Metropolitan and City of London Police, the various Railway Police forces and to the appropriate County Constabularies who had geographical jurisdiction along the Southampton to London railway line. It was a complete mystery as to where, how, when or by whom the crime had been perpetrated.

It is highly likely that the crime would have remained an unsolved mystery, had it not been for a 'hawk-eyed' young boy and the astute actions of a railway police constable who were involved in a sequence of events which later unfolded. During that Friday afternoon (9 May 1851), a boy, the son of a licenced victualler William Cross whose public house, the Eagle Tavern, was near Winchester railway station, was searching for birds' nests in some trees at the foot of a railway embankment near his home when he saw something concealed beneath a tree in a hedgerow. A closer inspection revealed it to be a wooden box which was very heavy. He struggled to carry the box but managed to take it home, where he handed it to his father who opened the box and revealed the contents. William Cross and his son then took the box to Winchester railway station and handed it to Police Constable Gadidge of the South Western Railway Police. The officer, who was aware of the missing gold shipment, accompanied the boy and his father to the place where the box had been found. The boy pointed to the spot beneath the tree where he had found the box. Police Constable Gadidge noticed that a large branch on the tree had been broken. Initially, he assumed that this had occurred as a result of the tree being struck by the heavy box as it rolled down the railway embankment. After a closer inspection however, the constable deduced that the box could not have landed in the exact spot where it had been found just by rolling down the embankment and he concluded that someone must have concealed it there. He suggested that an observation be carried out in case someone should return to retrieve it.

A police observation was mounted, which continued well into the evening. At about half past eleven, officers heard someone approaching the site. A man came to the spot where the box had been found earlier and appeared to be searching for it. The man was swiftly arrested and taken into custody.

The following morning, William Pamplin, a middle aged and respectably-attired man, who described himself a tailor, living in Earl Street, Shoreditch, London, was taken before the local Mayor and several other magistrates at Winchester Town Hall. Evidence was presented to the court regarding the theft of the gold, the finding of the box and subsequent arrest of the prisoner. Upon being arrested, the prisoner had told officers that he was lost and trying to find his way to the railway station.

The court heard that after his arrest, Pamplin was questioned by Detective Inspector Field of the South Western Railway Police and the name and address which he had given was verified as correct. During the interview, Pamplin stated that he had caught the one o'clock train from Waterloo that afternoon and travelled to Winchester looking for work. Enquiries revealed that there was no train to Winchester which left Waterloo at one o'clock. Furthermore, Pamplin was unable to supply information about anyone he had approached in relation to seeking employment. The prisoner protested his innocence to the Mayor who considered the circumstances before declaring that there was sufficient suspicion to remand the prisoner in custody pending further enquiries.

These revealed that a person matching the description of Pamplin was seen in Winchester on the evening of Thursday, 8 May, the day before his arrest. Mrs Lydia Cross, the wife of William Cross, the parents of the boy who found the wooden box, stated that she was working in the Eagle Tavern at about half past eleven in the evening, when a man matching the description of Pamplin entered the tap room of the pub and ordered a pint of beer. There was only one other customer in the tap room at the time, that being one Peter Pearce, a regular customer who was sleeping. She had never seen the customer before but as she served him, she noticed that he had in his possession a dark coloured shoulder bag which appeared to contain something bulky and heavy and he was also carrying a parcel measuring approximately 18in x 8in x 6in. He only remained in the pub for about fifteen minutes, leaving the premises at about a quarter to midnight, after he had consumed his ale. This evidence was corroborated by her daughter Eliza who was also present.

Two railway porters Mr Edwards and Mr Smith gave statements as to seeing a man of the same description arriving at Winchester station shortly before midnight to catch a train to London. This man was wearing a black shawl partially covering his face. He was carrying a dark navy or black shoulder bag which appeared to be heavy and under his arm was a parcel of the same description as that given by Mrs Cross.

Enquiries into this matter were also carried out in London. A statement was given to police by Mr Eldred, the proprietor of the Railway Coffee House in Shoreditch, East London, who stated that at about 5am on the morning on Friday, 9 May, a man arrived at the Coffee House from the South Western Railway by cab. The man had his face partially covered with a black shawl and was carrying a bag similar to the type used by lawyers and tied with a black cord. It appeared to contain something heavy. The man was also carrying a parcel about eighteen inches long. After partaking in a chop and coffee, he left the premises. On Saturday, 10 May, Mr Eldred accompanied Detective Constable Edward Funnell (City of London Police) to the county gaol at Winchester, where in the presence of Mr Barber, the prison Governor, and Superintendent Shepperd of the South Western Railway Police, Mr Eldred positively identified the prisoner Pamplin as the person who had come to his coffee shop on the Friday morning in question. Two dark blue bags and a black shawl were recovered from the home of Pamplin in Earl Street, during a search carried out by Detective Constable Funnell.

Pamplin was indicted to stand trial, and on 17 July 1851, he appeared before the western circuit of the Winchester Crown Court. Mr Justice Coleridge presided.

William Pamplin was indicted for having on the 9 May 1851, stolen 30 pounds weight of gold dust and a wooden box, valued at £1,000 (£146,000 today), the property of the South Western Railway Company. Another (alternative) count charged the prisoner with receiving the same, knowing or believing it to have been stolen.

Mr Rowe, Mr Montague Smith and Mr Phinn appeared for the prosecution, whilst Mr Butt QC and Mr C. Saunders defended the prisoner.

A summary of the evidence presented to the court as taken from newspaper quotes printed at the time reads as follows;

This case has been referred to as the 'Great Gold Dust Robbery'. The evidence for the prosecution having been adduced.

Mr Butt QC, in addressing the jury on behalf of the prisoner stated the following;

'A case of suspicion was not sufficient. There might be suspicion but there should be something far beyond that to induce a conviction. The ship arrived on the 7th and on the 8th was unloaded and these boxes were placed in a wagon. Not an enclosed wagon, but one merely covered with tarpaulins. The wagons then remained at the station for five hours, where all persons could have access to the place where the wagon remained. The jury should therefore look at the care or want of care which had been used. They must be aware of the facilities afforded to persons disposed to plunder. What protection had there been? No more than the company would have taken had the boxes been bullocks. A man could easily get in to the wagon. The persons who were to guard it were in the first-class carriage. Instead of taking care of the bullion, they were taking care of themselves. The jury had no evidence to show that the boxes ever left Southampton. The fact of the bullion being in the wagon was known to all the dock workers and all the persons employed on the railway'.

Mr Butt QC continued his address to the jury;

'The prisoner when apprehended gave his correct place of residence and also told the truth as to the public houses at which he had been. Had the prisoner been guilty, would he have done this? Would he not have given a false statement as to these particulars? The circumstance of the prisoner being in Winchester was not sufficient to induce them to come to the conclusion that the prisoner was guilty'.

Counsel submitted that the facts were not of such a nature as to call for a conviction.

Mr Justice Coleridge then summed up and went through all the evidence.

The jury retired for some time before returning with a verdict of not guilty to stealing the gold but guilty of receiving it, knowing or believing it to be stolen.

The prisoner said; 'All I can say is that I never had them in my possession. I never received one of them. I am as innocent as a child'.

Mr Justice Coleridge then addressed him; 'I have so very often heard persons in your situation affirm their innocence after their guilt has been most satisfactorily made out and established by the verdict of a jury. The observation you have made has no weight. There is no doubt my mind that you took a guilty part in this transaction. Few persons who have heard that evidence can entertain the slightest doubt. It might be a question whether you were a principal in the act of stealing, or whether you were a guilty receiver. It seems to me that the jury have drawn the right conclusion, that you did not take an active part in the stealing but that you were in the neighbourhood in concert with the persons who stole the boxes. When one considers that this was a crime most probably committed by many persons and there may have been the additional guilt of having corrupted some of the servants or other persons employed by the dock or railway company, it is impossible not to consider that it demands a severe punishment. The sentence is that you be transported for ten years.'

The trial had lasted nine hours.

William Pamplin was remanded in custody at Winchester prison and a date for his transportation was set for the 18 July that year.

After receiving news of his transportation date, William Pamplin requested a further interview with the authorities and was visited by police at Winchester prison. During an interview, he stated that although he had been convicted, he had taken no active part in the gold dust robbery and he had never handled any of the stolen gold. He further stated that the person seen in the Eagle Tavern and later by the two railway porters on the evening of the 8th was not him, nor was he the person who visited the coffee house belonging to Mr Eldred, even though he was confronted and identified by Mr Eldred whilst on remand in Winchester prison. He claimed that this was a genuine case of mistaken identity.

Pamplin went on to say that on the night of his arrest, although he had played no active part whatsoever in the stealing of the gold, he did visit the location where the box of gold had been concealed in order to retrieve it as he had been paid to do so. Upon his arrival at the spot where the box of gold should have been, he was arrested by police without even seeing the box. Consequently, after being arrested he denied all knowledge of the crime and even when he was charged and indicted to stand trial, he had no doubt in his mind that because he was an innocent man, 'justice would prevail' and he would be acquitted of both stealing and receiving the stolen gold. His conviction he stated was a miscarriage of justice.

It was only as a result of his wrongful conviction and threat of ten years transportation that he had decided to come clean and give a full and frank account of all that he knew about the robbery, in the hope that a review of his conviction would be carried out. He was assured that if he gave his full co-operation, a favourable review of his case would be considered.

Later, in a written confession, Pamplin stated that the robbery was planned by four men, during a meeting in the Three Crowns Tavern public house (also known by locals as the Black Dog), which was located in Crown Street, Hoxton, Shoreditch in East London.

The landlord of the public house was George Senior who was one of the men involved in the robbery. Also involved was a friend of his, Charles Whitcher. The person who had provided information about the gold shipment was William Winters. He was a former tallyman/porter with the South Western Railway Company who worked at the Nine Elms Goods Depot and who had been dismissed for misconduct some weeks earlier. Winters had claimed, that whilst working for the South-Western Railway Company, he had worked out a method whereby he could steal boxes of gold from the train, undetected and the loss would not be discovered until the train was unloaded at its destination. He did not go into any details about his plan.

The fourth gang member he stated was John Saward. He took part in the raid, but Pamplin was unable to say in what capacity. Pamplin said that he knew all the gang members and that he was offered a part in the robbery but had declined.

On Thursday, 8 May 1851, the train departed Southampton destined for London. One of the intermediate stops was Winchester where the train stopped for about ten minutes. It was at Winchester that the theft would take place. Pamplin assumed that Winters was able to board the train at Winchester without being seen and remove the gold from beneath the tarpaulin on one of the wagons. As the train departed Winchester, Winters was able to alight from the train with the gold in the vicinity of the Andover Road railway bridge. The train would have been travelling very slowly at this point.

The plan was for Winters to carry the three boxes of gold to Winchester railway station, where he would board a train and take the gold back to London. He wrapped one box up as a parcel and had taken a black shoulder bag with him for the other two boxes. Unfortunately, Winters found that only one box fitted in the bag and all three boxes were too big and too heavy for him to carry. He decided to take two boxes to London on the train as planned but he would hide the third box where it could be retrieved the following day. He concealed the box in a hedge at the foot of a tree adjacent the railway and he broke a branch on the tree to act as a marker for whoever collected it. This marker was the tree branch that railway constable Gadidge had wrongly assumed had been broken by the box as it rolled down the embankment.

Pamplin went on to say that it was in fact William Winters who Mrs Cross served with a pint of beer at the Eagle Tavern at half past eleven that evening and it was Winters who was seen by the porters Edwards and Smith as he went to the station with the gold to catch the train to London.

Upon arrival in London, William Winters did take a cab from the railway station to Shoreditch where he stopped off at Mr Eldred's coffee-house for an early breakfast before taking the stolen boxes to the Three Crowns Tavern and handing them to George Senior.

Mr Eldred was later re-interviewed by police and gave a further statement stating that he may have made a mistake when identifying Pamplin in prison due to the man having his face partially covered by a scarf whilst in his coffee shop.

Pamplin went on to say that later that morning, he was present in the Three Crowns Tavern when Winters explained to the other gang members what had happened in Winchester the previous evening. He said that everything was fine and produced a map which he had drawn showing where the third box was concealed and he mentioned the tree with the broken branch under which the box was hidden. Mr Witcher said that he would go and retrieve the box but demanded an extra twenty pounds for doing so. It was at this point that Pamplin intervened and offered to do the job for ten pounds, which was agreed by the gang. It was whilst attempting to retrieve the box, that he was arrested.

Pamplin was asked by the police why he had taken such a big risk for the sum of ten pounds. He stated that had he been successful in recovering the box, it was his intention to keep the box himself and offer to sell it back to the gang members for £600, half of its estimated worth.

As a result of the information supplied by Pamplin, police began to arrest the gang members who had actually planned and executed the raid. The suspect William Winters evaded capture and his whereabouts became unknown.

Winters wife, Sally, was arrested at her brother's house in Buxton Place, West Ham by Police Constable Addington of the Metropolitan Police, K Division, after 200 gold sovereigns and a gold watch and chain were found hidden under her brother's bed. She admitted receiving the items from her husband William and further admitted that the 200 sovereigns were realized from a portion of the stolen gold dust. Later she admitted to receiving other items of stolen property, including boxes of silk stockings, scarves, gloves, shawls and rolls of silk which had been stolen by her husband whilst he was employed by the South Western Railway Company. She also stated that other items of stolen goods had passed through her house after being delivered there by a Mr Chaplin and a Mr Horne, on their delivery cart. This property was also believed to have been stolen by her husband William from the railway depot at Nine Elms.

Charles Whitcher, a greengrocer, was arrested at his home at 14, Church Row, Aldgate, East London and John Saward, a linen draper of Hereford Place, Commercial Road East, Aldgate, London was also arrested on suspicion of being involved the great gold dust robbery and receiving stolen silk.

Charles Whitcher, George Senior and John Saward were charged with stealing the three boxes of gold dust from the South Western Railway Company. They appeared before Wandsworth Magistrates Court in London on the 26 August 1851 and were committed to stand trial at the Central Criminal Court (Old Bailey). No evidence was offered against Mrs Sally Winters, who had been charged with receiving stolen property.

William Pamplin gave evidence against the three defendants at their trial when they appeared before the Old Bailey. Each of them was convicted of stealing the three boxes of gold dust and sentenced as follows. Charles Whitcher to ten years transportation. George Senior to seven years transportation but his transportation was never imposed, due to his sudden death on the 14 November 1851, resulting from bronchitis and inflammation of the windpipe. He was forty years of age. John Saward was sentenced to twelve months imprisonment.

William Winters evaded capture and was believed to have fled to America, where he spent the rest of his life on the run, separated from his wife and family. Had he been apprehended and convicted for his involvement in the crime, there is little doubt that he would have been sentenced to a minimum of ten years transportation, due to him being one of the key members of the gang and having played the most active part in the commission of the crime by using inside knowledge which he had gained from his former employer, the South Western Railway Company.

After giving evidence against the gang, William Pamplin was granted a Free Pardon by the Home Office on the grounds of continued ill health and was released from Winchester County prison on Wednesday, 17 March 1852.

What happened to the stolen gold dust?

The box of gold dust found by Cross and recovered intact was returned to the owner. The remaining two boxes of gold dust which were taken from Winchester to London by William Winters were never recovered, having been sold on by George Senior. He never divulged to whom he sold the gold, but it is thought that he received in the region of £4,000 for it (over £586,000 today). The exact amount of money which he received was never established.

George Senior paid the sum of fifty guineas to Mr Butt QC to represent Pamplin after his arrest. George also paid the sum of thirty shillings a week to Mrs Mary Pamplin, the wife of William Pamplin who lived in East Street, Finsbury, during the period of his incarceration. The house she lived in was tenanted by her husband.

Senior also advanced the sum of £600 (£88,000 today) to William Winters to aid his escape, out of which Winters gave his wife the 200 gold sovereigns.

It is assumed that the remaining money was shared between Senior and Whitcher. It is not known whether William Winters was given any additional money after he went on the run, or whether he had any further contact with the other gang members. As previously stated, the missing gold dust was never recovered.

In December 1851, a civil action was brought before the Court of the Exchequer (an English appellate court which existed at that time until abolished in 1873). The case was brought by Rothschild and others, against the Royal Mail Steam-Packet Company. Lord Chief Baron presided. Details of the civil claim were as follows. It was stated that the defendants were contracted to bring a number of boxes containing gold dust from Panama and to safely deliver them to the Bank of England in London which they failed to do.

Claim:- On the 7 May, in the present year, a steamer belonging to the defendant called the SS *Great Western*, arrived at Southampton with 283 boxes of gold dust, of which eleven belonged to the plaintiffs, Messrs Rothschild. The boxes were placed in wagons on the South Western Railway for the purpose of being conveyed to London. When at Winchester, the train stopped for about ten minutes and it was there that three boxes were supposed to have been stolen. One of the boxes belonged to the plaintiffs, the value of which they sought in the present action to recover. When the train arrived at Nine Elms, the robbery was discovered.

Sir Frederick Thesiger, 1st Baron of Chelmsford addressed the jury for the defendants, and said that he should be able to show that the robbery had not taken place from the steamer, in which they were brought over and placed in the wagons which conveyed them to London. He would show that they left Southampton Docks perfectly safe and it was most likely that the robbery was committed whist the train was in motion. He (Sir Frederick Thesiger) would also show that four servants of the Royal Mail Steam- Packet Company had travelled up to London in the train containing the gold dust and that the greatest care had been exercised by them in watching the wagons in which the boxes containing the gold dust were placed. He therefore submitted that the defendants had not been guilty of any negligence and were not liable to the plaintiffs.

Lord Chief Baron in his summing up stated that the defendants were contracted to deliver the boxes of gold dust to London and he left it to the jury to decide whether there had been any negligence on the part of the defendants. The jury returned a verdict for the plaintiffs (Rothschild and others).

As a result of the great gold dust robbery, as it was dubbed in newspapers of the day, the South Western Railway Company took immediate action to prevent any repeat of this sort of crime.

It was reported by the press in May 1852:

The South Western Railway Company has now placed wagons on their line, built expressly for the conveyance of specie [money in the form of coins rather than notes]. These carriages are built of iron and they enclose the specie completely. They are secured by special bolts and locks. Purpose built bullion vans had been introduced onto the railways in Britain for the first time.

Most people have heard of the Great Train Robbery which was carried out in 1963 but few have heard of the Great Gold Dust Robbery of 1851, although technically, the crime carried out was not by definition one of robbery, but that of larceny at the time (theft today). It was indeed a well-planned, and a well-executed operation. Had it not been for a twist of fate, it may well have gone undetected.

Thieves Target North London Goods Depot

On 18 May 1847, John Freer, aged 28, William Martin aged 25, and Henry East aged 20, all described as labourers, appeared before the Central Criminal Court in London, charged with stealing a large quantity of silks, drapery and other valuable items which were in transit on the London and North Western Railway. Also appearing before the Court were Samuel Freer aged 27, John Cherry aged 28, Joseph Taylor aged 27 and Charles Austin aged 37, each of whom was charged with receiving stolen property from Freer, Martin and East.

The Court heard that on Easter Sunday, 4 April 1847, Freer, Martin and East decided to enter the London and North Western Goods Depot at Camden Town in order to steal property from the covered wagons and vans which were stabled there. Easter Sunday was specifically chosen because the men were aware that no staff would be working that night due it being a Bank Holiday. There was however one railway policeman on duty at the depot during the night and the men planning the raid were aware of this. The goods depot itself covered a large area, with nine different railway lines inside the depot. These lines contained well over 100 trucks laden with all manner of goods which formed several trains stabled in different parts of the depot. It was the duty of the policeman to continually patrol the depot during his twelve-hour shift, checking that all the wagons and vans were securely fastened and their contents intact, as well as keeping his eyes and ears focused for any potential intruders within the depot. The thieves, who had done their homework in planning the raid, knew that when the constable checked a particular part of the depot, it would normally take him at least a couple of hours before he returned to the same location on his next patrol. This would allow ample time to raid one or more of the vans, with little chance of being interrupted.

The gang were also aware of the different type of goods which were on hand in the depot and certainly knew what they were looking for. The 'Up goods trains' contained mostly hardware and similar goods manufactured in the industrial centres of Birmingham and Sheffield, which had been sent to the Camden Town depot for distribution in London and the South East. The 'Down goods trains' however tended to contain more valuable items including silks, fine linen, glass, porcelain and good quality articles which had been manufactured locally and were awaiting transportation to the Midlands, the North of England and Scotland. These were the vans which the gang would ultimately target.

Freer, Martin and East entered the depot shortly after two o'clock in the morning and established the whereabouts of the patrolling policeman, before targeting a row of vans. They selected a van which contained items being sent from local firm Messrs Weaver and Co. The men lay in wait beneath some wagons until the constable had examined the row of vans and moved on. After ensuring that the coast was clear, the men forced their way into the vehicle and started to unload the contents. They removed a large quantity of woollen blankets, drapery, rolls of velvet, shawls, gloves, silk, ribbon and other articles valued at £700 (£76,000 today). The men carried the stolen property to the perimeter of the depot where they had a horse and cart waiting to take the items away. They loaded the stolen property onto the cart and made good their escape. The railway policeman did not discover the pilfered van until later that morning, by which time the gang were long gone.

The stolen property was taken by horse and cart to a smallholding in Camden not far from the goods depot where it was concealed in a pigsty. There it remained hidden until it was moved to a beer-shop in Peckham the following Tuesday. The beer-shop was owned by Samuel Freer, the brother of John Freer. Initially, Samuel was reluctant to accept the stolen property from his brother, but he was eventually persuaded by John to store the goods in the cellar of his shop until they could be disposed of. During the next few days, John Cherry, Joseph Taylor and Charles Austin made several visits to the shop to collect the stolen property.

Meanwhile, a 19 year old youth, Joseph Page, had been arrested by police in connection with another matter and he was remanded in custody. Whilst incarcerated, Page supplied details to the police about the three men who had carried out the raid at the Camden Goods Depot on the Easter Sunday. Freer, Martin and East were swiftly arrested. These arrests were soon followed by the arrests of the remainder of the men who had knowingly received property stolen from the railway. All of the men subsequently admitted the charges against them and pleaded guilty when they appeared in court.

'Having been found guilty,' the Recorder in passing sentence said that the prisoners had been convicted of a very bold and alarming depredation and he felt it his duty to sentence John Freer, Henry East, William Martin, John Cherry, Joseph Taylor and Charles Austin to seven years transportation. He went on to say that the other prisoner, Samuel Freer, appeared to have acted by a desire to screen and protect his brother John and he did not take any share of the plunder. On these grounds, the Court felt justified in sentencing him to twelve months imprisonment with hard labour. The prisoners were removed from the dock.

Stealing goods in transit from the railway was extremely common during the nineteenth century and cost the railway companies millions of pounds in lost revenue. It was also a highly lucrative trade for both career criminals and some dishonest railway staff who were often the main culprits in this type of crime. Various methods ranging from re-labelling packages to organised gang raids in remote railway siding and goods depots were frequently used to steal items in transit. This resulted in the Railway Companies setting up goods claims departments to deal with the increasing numbers of claims from customers for non-receipt of goods which had been stolen in transit. These claims departments paid out vast sums of money on a regular basis to affected customers, often with little or no proper investigation due to the sheer volume of claims being processed. Railway companies were in a constant battle to combat the serious problem of goods being stolen whilst in transit upon the railway.

The problem continued throughout the nineteenth and early twentieth centuries when almost all the goods and freight in Britain was transported by railway companies. From the late 1950s, extensive motorways and new roads were built in Britain which resulted in the creation of road haulage companies which led to the gradual decline of goods and freight being transported by rail and by the twenty-first century, the vast majority of goods and freight was being transported by road.

'Bent' Solicitor Sent to Prison

Edward Stanley Bent, a Manchester solicitor, appeared before Manchester Assizes in March 1878, charged with having feloniously received from a thief, whom he had represented in court on several occasions, two portmanteaus (large leather travelling bags), containing watches, jewellery and clothing, the personal property of two individuals, Mr Parnell MP and Mr Harry Prosser. Mr Hopwood QC, MP conducted the prosecution and Mr Higgins QC defended Bent who pleaded not guilty.

The court heard that a person by the name of Franklin, a notorious railway thief, had stolen the property in question from a railway station in Manchester. He was subsequently arrested and tried at the Manchester Quarter Sessions the previous August and convicted.

The prisoner, Edward Stanley Bent had represented Franklin and after the conviction attended Franklin's lodgings, where the two portmanteaus were given to him. A search warrant was later obtained by Police Inspector McCelland and the two portmanteaus, one of which bore Mr Parnell's name, were found in Edward Bent's office. The contents had been partially removed, including some valuable jewellery. Bent said that he had received the property as payment for defending Franklin and he denied knowing that it had been stolen.

Mr Parnell MP, the owner of one of the portmanteaus recovered, gave evidence in which he identified the bag as his property, stating that it had been stolen from him whilst he was travelling by train from Leeds to Manchester to attend a meeting. Despite protesting his innocence, the trial jury later returned a verdict of guilty against Edward Bent in relation to the charge of knowingly receiving stolen goods. The judge sentenced Bent to five years' penal servitude, stating that he was a disgrace to his profession.

Goods Stolen between England and Scotland

In 1854, the Caledonian Railway Company and the Glasgow and South Western Railway Company both began to receive numerous complaints about losses of goods in transit in both directions between England and Scotland. It was not known where the thefts were taking place, as the stolen items were being transported over both railway networks as well as other networks belonging to a number of different railway companies, in some cases hundreds of miles apart.

In order to solve these crimes, it became vital for the railway police to establish exactly where these offences were occurring. In order to achieve this, a detailed exchange of information took place between various railway police forces of all goods lost or stolen in transit, together with the names of places where the losses were likely to have occurred.

In order to try to stamp out this type of crime, Police Superintendent E.J. Brierley was appointed head of a special task force which was set up to investigate these losses. The unit consisted of officers selected from five different railway police forces, namely the Glasgow and South Western railway police, the Caledonian Railway police, the Lancaster and Carlisle railway police, the London and North Western railway police, and the Lancashire and Yorkshire railway police.

For several months, officers belonging to the task force travelled the railway network, collating information about specific goods and other property which were reported missing in transit, whilst at the same time observing the movements and practices of railway staff who had access to the missing goods. Eventually, a pattern began to emerge which revealed that most of the losses seemed to be centred on Carlisle in Cumbria, involving trains travelling in both directions from Glasgow to Carlisle and Carlisle to Preston. This area became the focus of attention and after several more weeks, Superintendent Brierley and his team had compiled a list of suspects, mainly train guards working for the Lancaster and Carlisle Railway, whom he suspected were responsible for stealing items of goods in transit.

On Monday, 21 May 1855, Superintendent Brierley visited the home of Edward Caton, a train guard employed by the Lancaster and Carlisle Railway Company who lived in Back Saul Street, Preston but Caton was not at home. Superintendent Brierley carried out a search of the premises where he lived and in an upstairs bedroom, he found a large box which was locked. He broke open the box and found it to contain numerous articles which he suspected had been stolen from the railway. One of the items was a roll of moiré fabric which was later identified as having been stolen in transit. Later, Superintendent Brierley returned to the house, accompanied by Sergeant Pool. On this occasion, they found Caton hiding in a coal cupboard under the stairs. He was arrested on suspicion of stealing from the railway but stated that he could prove that he had bought most of items in question.

Also on 21 May, Superintendent Brierley and Sergeant Pool visited the home of John Butler, also a train guard on the Lancaster and Carlisle railway.

He resided at Hudson Street Preston. Butler was not at home, so they spoke to his mother-in-law. A search of that house was made and a number of silk handkerchiefs were recovered from the front room downstairs, together with some items believed to have been stolen from luggage belonging to Mr Jardine, a railway passenger.

On 21 February 1855, Mr Jardine, a banker had travelled by train from Scotland to Chatham via Carlisle and London. He changed trains at Carlisle and travelled in a first class compartment from Carlisle to London. His suitcase was placed in the luggage section of the guard's van at Carlisle in the care of the train guard. After arriving home, he found that his suitcase had been tampered with. The following items were missing from the suitcase; a necktie with two gold tie pins in it, one diamond pin and one pearl pin, valued at twelve guineas (£1,200 today), together with a razor strop. The razor strop and tie pins were amongst the items recovered from Butler's house, along with some staff timetables of freight train movements on the Lancaster and Carlisle Railway. Butler was formally arrested by Sergeant Pool.

Superintendent Brierley then travelled to Glasgow where he searched a house belonging to Joseph Birrell, who was employed as a platelayer on the Caledonian Railway. More silk handkerchiefs were recovered. Birrell failed to give an account as to how they came into his possession, so he was arrested and taken into custody.

Police Constable Lockwood, another officer from Superintendent Brierley's team, arrested Joseph Birrell Jnr (son of Joseph Birrell Snr), a train guard employed by the Lancaster and Carlisle railway, at his home in Glasgow. A search of his house revealed a large box containing a variety of goods including more silk handkerchiefs. Birrell admitted the box and contents were his, but he refused to say where the contents of the box had come from, other than that he had brought them in Carlisle the previous night.

On the 26 May, Police Constable Hyslop, also serving under the command of Superintendent Brierley, visited the home of William Birrell (brother of Joseph Birrell) at an address in Stanwix, Carlisle. William was at home with his wife and child. Also in the house was his wife's mother, brother and sister, who were all living there. PC Hyslop recovered nine silk handkerchiefs and other items which he believed were stolen. William Birrell was also taken into custody.

It will be noted that quite a few silk handkerchiefs were recovered from the homes of defendants during this enquiry. Although of no great monetary value, these were an important aspect in this case, due to the fact that they were included in a list of items of stolen property held by Superintendent Brierley, who was in possession of written statements, previously obtained by his officers during the initial stages of the enquiry, proving that the silk handkerchiefs seized during the searches were stolen whilst in transit upon the railway under the following circumstances:

On Saturday 24 March 1855, a consignment of two boxes, each containing 366 silk handkerchiefs (10 packs of 36) were sent by train from Messrs Macaulay and Co, St. Vincent's Lane, Glasgow, to Messrs Brunel and Co, Liverpool.

Robert Baird, a foreman employed by Messrs James Macaulay and Co, gave a statement to police, describing the handkerchiefs in detail and confirming the packing and despatch of the two boxes from the factory in Glasgow.

Thomas Anderson, a carter employed by Pickford and Co (hauliers), gave a statement to police which confirmed that he received the parcels from Baird and conveyed them to the Glasgow and South Western Railway Company goods depot in Glasgow, where he handed them to George Gibson, a goods porter. Porter Gibson confirmed receipt of the items which he later placed into parcels van number 822 on a train to Liverpool.

The train departed Glasgow for Liverpool at 6.20pm, arriving in Carlisle at about 1am the following morning. Police Constable William Blaskett, employed by the Lancaster and Carlisle Railway Police, met the train upon its arrival at Carlisle. Part of his duties that night consisted of checking all the vans on the train (including van number 822) when it arrived from Glasgow, which he did. All the vans and contents appeared to be secure and intact. The train was then shunted from the Caledonian Railway into sidings which belonged to the Lancaster and Carlisle Railway Company, where it remained until 6.50am when it departed for Liverpool.

The train stopped at Preston and just prior to its departure, a silk handkerchief was found on the floor of van number 822 by a member of staff, indicating that the parcel had either been damaged, or interfered with between Carlisle and Preston. The train continued to Liverpool Waterloo Station where Thomas Watson, a goods porter employed by the London and North Western Railway Company, unloaded the van. He also found a silk handkerchief on the floor of the van and handed it to John Court, the warehouse man.

Edward Jones, a carter for the London and North Western Railway Company, conveyed the two cartons to Messrs Brunel and Co and handed them to Mr Henry Banks. He remarked that one of the boxes was extremely light. Messrs Brunel later reported that the box referred to by Banks as being light, was in fact empty and the 360 silk handkerchiefs were missing from it.

On 29 May, Sergeant Pool had a conversation with John Butler who made an unexpected confession. Butler said he had travelled (worked) with William Birrell on several occasions and it was Birrell who had first caused him to take anything. After that, when Birrell stole something, he would leave stolen property in the van for him (Butler), who had to take it, otherwise it would have been found by the authorities. After that, Butler started to take things himself and leave some behind in the van for Birrell in the same way that Birrell had left things for him. Later he got bolder and just took things which he kept for himself. He said he had been doing this for the past few years. He further stated that if he had never met Birrell, he would never have got involved. Butler's brother Henry was present when the conversation took place.

On Wednesday, 13 June 1855, five men, Joseph Birrell Snr, William Birrell, Joseph Birrell Jnr, John Butler, Edwards Caton, all employed in the capacity of train guards with the Lancaster and Carlisle Railway were committed by local magistrates to stand trial at the Lancaster Assize Court.

On Friday, 10 November that year, the defendants appeared before Mr Justice Crowder at the Lancaster Assizes. Mr James QC and Mr Bagot QC appeared for the prosecution. Mr Wigham QC and Mr Cross QC represented the prisoners.

All three Birrells and John Butler were charged with stealing the 360 silk handkerchiefs belonging to the Lancaster and Carlisle Railway Company. Joseph Birrell Snr also faced an alternative charge of handling stolen handkerchiefs. They all pleaded not guilty. John Butler faced an additional charge, of stealing two gold tie pins and a razor strop belonging to Mr Jardine. He pleaded not guilty. Edward Caton was charged with stealing a piece of moiré antique fabric belonging to the Lancaster and Carlisle Railway Company. He pleaded not guilty. The case against each of the defendants was heard, after which, the jury retired to consider their verdicts. After just a short deliberation, the verdicts were announced.

Joseph Birrell Snr was found not guilty on the charge of stealing silk handkerchiefs, but was found guilty of receiving them, knowing them to have been stolen. Joseph Birrell Jnr, his brother William Birrell and John Butler were each found guilty of stealing the silk handkerchiefs. John Butler was also found guilty of stealing the gold tie pins and the razor strop belonging to Mr Jardine and Edward Caton was found guilty of stealing the moiré antique fabric.

After the verdicts had been announced, Mr Justice Crowder addressed the court to pass sentence. He said that he entirely agreed with the verdict of the jury. He stated that all the defendants were in the employ of the railway companies, receiving competent wages and it was their duty to look after property intrusted into their care. With respect to Joseph Birrell Snr, he had been convicted of receiving the stolen goods and it was highly probable that by his bad example, his sons were induced to commit these crimes. It was absolutely necessary that in cases of this kind, an example should be made. The luggage of all passengers must be carried safely on the railway and it was sometimes necessary to protect the public. The judge then sentenced each of the defendants to serve four years penal servitude. The prisoners were removed from the dock.

A large quantity of other items believed to have been stolen by the defendants from the railway and subsequently recovered from their homes was not subject to any further charges, due to the fact that the items were never claimed and the owners could not be traced.

The special task force headed by Superintendent Brierley had achieved its aim but was then disbanded. As railway companies became more efficient, stringent checks were made on goods in transit and more records were kept. Each company checked consignments as they entered and left their jurisdiction, which gave a better indication as to where any thefts of goods in transit were taking place and a regular exchange of information was maintained between the various railway police authorities. Unfortunately, as long as the railways carry goods, crimes of this nature will continue.

Railway Sleepers Stolen

On Monday, 19 December 1887, Alexander Hay and Stewart Fisken entered Balhousie railway sidings, in St Catherine's Road, Perth and stole ten railway sleepers. They were subsequently arrested and pleaded guilty when they appeared in court. Hay was sentenced to six months imprisonment and Fisken received two months imprisonment.

Jewellery Stolen from Train

On Wednesday, 18 July 1894, Frederick Foster aged 26, was sentenced to five years penal servitude after pleading guilty to stealing jewellery from luggage vans on the Midland Railway at Nottingham. He had been apprehended by railway detectives following complaints from passengers of missing items from their baggage.

Greedy Shunter Stole a Bottle of Wine

George Greedy, a shunter employed by the Rhymney Railway Company in South Wales was sentenced to four months imprisonment with hard labour for stealing a bottle of wine from a railway wagon on Wednesday, 18 June 1873. Greedy, who had no previous convictions, was told by the magistrate that the severity of sentence was a warning to others.

Railway Warehouse Broken Into

On Sunday, 4 June 1893, a railway constable was on routine patrol at Gainsborough when he apprehended James White, aged 27, after observing him break into a warehouse belonging to the Manchester, Sheffield and Lincolnshire railway. White did not resist arrest and admitted to the constable that he was looking for something to steal to make a few shillings. He was sentenced to four months imprisonment with hard labour.

The First Great Train Robbery

The first Great Train Robbery, also referred to as the Great Gold Robbery, took place in May 1855, when £14,000 worth of gold bullion (almost £1.6 million today), was stolen from a train which was travelling from London to Folkestone. The consignment was destined for Paris.

Fishing boats and trading vessels have been using the shores of Folkestone in Kent since roman times. At the beginning of the nineteenth century, it was decided to build a harbour, in part to be used by naval warships engaged in the Napoleonic Wars. The Folkestone Harbour Company was established and two stone piers designed by Thomas Telford were constructed to provide a safe haven for vessels.

Building of the two piers was completed in 1820, after which, plans to complete the rest of the harbour complex was put on hold due to lack of finance. The harbour was never finished, and the Folkestone Harbour Company was declared bankrupt in 1842.

The South Eastern Railway Company then purchased the harbour and surrounding land in order to develop the site into a cross channel ferry terminal for steamships to operate between Folkestone and Boulogne in Northern France. At that time, the railway company was also developing the port of Dover some ten miles away, to operate ferry services to Calais in France and Ostend in Belgium. A new railway station was built at Folkestone Harbour in 1843 to handle freight traffic before being opened to passenger traffic in 1850. From 1850 onwards, regular boat train services were being operated by the South Eastern Railway Company from London Bridge railway station to both Folkestone and Dover to connect with cross-channel ferry services to the continent.

Throughout the 1850s, a combined train and boat connecting service from London to Paris via Folkestone and Boulogne ran four times daily, at 8am, 11.30am and 4.30pm with one night time service at 8.30pm. The trains and packet steamers carried all types of cargo including the royal mail, as well as conveying passengers. The service also carried valuable commodities such as the gold bullion which was to become the target for a gang of thieves intent on stealing it.

In the spring of 1855, 38-year-old William Pierce, a petty criminal from London, approached Edward Agar, aged about 40, who he knew to be a professional career criminal, having spent his entire life engaged in criminal pursuits. Pierce informed Agar that, as a former railway employee who had been dismissed from the South Eastern Railway Company for misconduct, he had inside information on how to steal a shipment of gold bullion being transported between London and Paris. He told Agar that he was unable to steal the bullion alone as it required the expertise of a professional. Agar immediately showed an interest and the two men agreed to meet again to discuss the matter in more detail.

Pierce later outlined his plan to Agar. He informed Agar that periodically, shipments of gold were sent from bullion merchants in London to the Bank of France in Paris on the overnight cross-channel service which departed with a boat train leaving London Bridge at 8.30pm bound for Folkestone and Dover. The bullion was transferred at Folkestone to the night ferry service which operated to Boulogne. The final leg of the journey was by train to Gare du Nord railway station in Paris. Pierce told Agar that he still kept in touch with a few former friends and working colleagues on the railway and it would not difficult for him to find out when these shipments of bullion were taking place.

The gold bullion, he said, was packed into wooden bullion boxes, secured with metal bands. In turn, these wooden boxes were weighed at London Bridge Station before departure, then placed inside three identical 'strongboxes' which were sometimes referred to as railway safes or travelling safes. These strongboxes were made of iron and manufactured by the Chubb Lock and Safe Company in London. Each strongbox was 3ft (91.44cm) square and they were transported in the guard's van of the train under the constant watchful eye of the train guard. The strongboxes in question were hinged on the inside with lids on top, which could be raised to gain access. Each of the strongboxes also had two built-in locks with separate keyholes. The twin locks required two different keys to open them, although the same pair of keys did open all three strongboxes.

The strongboxes were transferred from the boat train at Folkestone, onto a cross channel packet steamer, also owned by the South Eastern Railway Company. Upon arrival at Boulogne, they were unlocked and opened by the ship's captain, the wooden bullion boxes removed and weighed again before being handed over to the French authorities who transferred them onto a train bound for Paris.

In order to open the strongboxes, several sets of two keys were available. The first set of keys was secured in a locked cabinet at South Eastern Railway offices at London Bridge Station. A second set was held by a senior railway official working inside the booking office at Folkestone and several other sets were in the possession of the captains of various South Eastern Railway vessels, operating the cross Channel ferry service.

Pierce went on to tell Agar that he knew a senior railway guard by the name of James Burgess who regularly worked the boat trains between London Bridge, Folkestone and Dover, who would be prepared to assist in stealing the gold bullion if the raid was carried out on a day when he was working the train which was transporting it. Burgess had worked as a guard for over ten years and was a trusted employee, who would not arouse suspicion. Agar said that in his opinion, it would not be possible to open the strongboxes in transit and remove the gold without having a set of keys but Pierce told him he had thought of a way around that.

Pierce went on to say that another South Eastern railway employee, William Tester worked as a railway clerk in the South Eastern Railway office in London where one set of the strongbox keys were stored and he may be able to gain access to them briefly, if Agar was able to copy them to make a set of duplicates. Agar said that may be possible, so the plan was put into action. Burgess and Tester were approached by Pierce and both agreed to take part in the raid.

Agar later visited a public house in Tooley Street, London, not far from the workplace of William Tester. At a pre-arranged time, after unlocking the key cabinet and removing the safe keys, Tester was able to slip out of his office for a few minutes to meet Agar. The two men met briefly, and Tester handed one of the safe keys to Agar who made a wax impression of it in order to create a duplicate. Unfortunately, Tester who was very nervous told Agar that the second key in his possession was not the other safe key, as he had removed the wrong key from the locked cabinet whilst in a state of panic. He told Agar that if he managed to get away with it on this occasion, he was not prepared to do it all again to get the second safe key as he was afraid of being caught. Tester then returned to work and returned the keys to the cabinet, fortunately for him without arousing any suspicions.

Agar and Pierce decided that if they were to continue with the plan, they would have to obtain an impression of the other safe key elsewhere but needed to find out where it was kept. After giving the matter a great deal of thought, Agar came up with an ingenious idea. He visited the South Eastern Railway offices in London where he gave his name as Mr Archer, a gentleman, who wanted a box of gold sovereigns securely transported from London to Folkestone by train in one of their strongboxes, to be collected upon arrival. The railway company agreed to transport the box of sovereigns and a few days later a securely sealed wooden bullion box purporting to contain gold sovereigns, but in fact containing scrap iron, was transported by train in a strongbox to Folkestone where Mr 'Archer' was waiting to collect it. The strong box was removed from the train, placed on a barrow and taken to the booking office by two railway porters. Agar was waiting at the booking office to ensure that his box was secure when it was removed from the strongbox. Agar watched closely as the chief booking clerk went into the back room of the booking office and removed the safe keys from a cupboard. The safe was opened and the wooden box which supposedly contained gold sovereigns was handed intact to Mr 'Archer'.

Having established the whereabouts of the keys, Agar and Pierce later visited Folkestone, at a quiet time of day when just one booking clerk was on duty in the office. Pierce approached the booking office window and made enquiries with the clerk about train times and fare prices. In the meantime, whilst the booking clerk was busy attending to Pierce, Agar was able to open the door of the booking office unobserved and slip into the back room. As he approached the cupboard containing the strong-box keys he could hardly believe his luck. The key to the cupboard was still in the lock. He quickly opened the cupboard, identified the second strong-box key and made a wax impression of it. He left the booking office unnoticed, whilst Pierce was still in conversation with the booking clerk. Both Agar and Pierce had been extremely daring and enterprising in their actions in order to obtain an impression of the second key, but lady luck was on their side and they had got away with it. They were now well and truly ready to put the next stage of their plan into operation.

The next time Pierce contacted Agar was to inform him that a consignment of gold bullion weighing 224lb (102kg) was being transported in three strongboxes from London to Paris on the 8.30pm boat train departing from London Bridge Station on 15 May 1885 and that James Burgess was rostered to be the train guard.

Both Agar and Pierce visited the Lambeth Lead Factory in London, on separate occasions, where they collectively purchased 224lb of lead shot (small balls/pellets of lead for use in shotgun cartridges). The lead was to be used to replace the gold bullion being stolen from the wooden boxes to ensure that the weight of the boxes at Boulogne remained the same as it was when the boxes were weighed in London.

Agar and Pierce were ready to put the final stages of their clever plan into action. At about 8.15pm on Tuesday, 15 May 1855, the two men both arrived at London Bridge Station in a hansom cab, dressed as gentlemen and carrying luggage bags. They booked first class tickets to Dover and walked along the station platform towards the train. They handed their luggage bags to a porter, requesting that they be stored in the guard's van until they reached their destination.

The porter, unaware that the bags contained lead shot, took them to the guard's van and handed them to Burgess who placed them inside his van where the three Chubb strongboxes had already been loaded. Just prior to the departure of the train, Pierce entered a first class carriage whilst Burgess who was standing by the door of the guards van, allowed Agar to slip past him into the guards van unnoticed. At 8.30pm precisely Burgess waved his green flag, blew his whistle and the boat-train left the station bound for Folkestone and Dover.

As soon as the train cleared the station. Agar got to work. He opened one of the three strongboxes with the duplicate keys which he had made earlier from the wax impressions. As expected, the strongbox contained a wooden bullion box secured by metal bands. With a hammer and chisel which had been concealed in one of his travel bags, Agar removed the metal bands from the box, opened it and took out the gold bullion. He replaced the bullion with lead shot before securing the box and slipping the metal bands back over it. He replaced the bullion box back inside the strong-box and locked it.

Shortly afterwards, the train arrived at Redhill Station which was the first station stop. It had been pre-arranged that William Tester would meet the train at Redhill and take his share of the gold bullion back to London. As the train pulled into the station, Pierce alighted from his first class carriage and joined Tester on the station platform. They both walked to the guard's van. Pierce quickly entered the guards van unobserved whilst Agar slipped a gold bar into a bag that Tester was carrying. Tester remained on the station platform until the train departed, before catching the first train back to London. The boat-train continued its journey.

As the boat-train travelled south, Agar and Pierce opened the other two strong-boxes and began removing gold from the bullion boxes, replacing it with lead shot. The wooden bullion boxes were secured with their metal bands and put back into the strongboxes which were then locked. The gold bullion was placed in the luggage bags belonging to Agar and Pierce, where it would remain until the train arrived at its final destination in Dover.

Upon arrival at Folkestone, Pierce and Agar hid behind some luggage and parcels in the guard's van whilst guard Burgess supervised the unloading of the three strongboxes from his guards van onto a barrow which was standing on the station platform being escorted by two railway policemen. The strongboxes were escorted to the quayside before being loaded aboard the steamship *Lord Warden*, destined for Boulogne.

As the boat train was about to depart Folkestone, Pierce and Agar alighted from the guard's van and entered a first class carriage to continue their journey to Dover. Upon arrival at Dover, they returned to the guard's van where Burgess handed them their travel bags (full of gold bullion) and they left the station, making their way to a nearby ale house for refreshments. The two men toasted their success before returning to London on a boat-train from

Dover, which was carrying passengers who had arrived by ferry from Ostend in Belgium. To avoid arousing any suspicion when they passed through the ticket barrier at London Bridge station after leaving a boat-train carrying passengers arriving from Ostend, they were both in possession of return portions of London to Ostend railway tickets which they had purchased in London several days earlier. Every meticulous detail it seemed had been planned to perfection by Agar who was indeed an accomplished professional criminal. It appeared that a perfect crime had been planned and executed by a gang of men who were now extremely wealthy individuals.

On Wednesday, 16 May 1855, the wooden bullion boxes which should have contained gold bullion were opened at a bank in Paris by bank cashier Pierre Heznard. To his utter amazement, he discovered that the bullion had been stolen and replaced with lead shot. Police were summoned and senior railway officials of the South Eastern Railway Company in London were immediately advised, so too were officials of the French Railways and the bullion merchants who had dispatched the consignments from London. Enquiries were launched by the South Eastern Railway Police and the Metropolitan Police in London as well as the police authorities in France. Three bullion dealers from the City of London, namely Messrs Built, Messrs Speilmann and Abell & Co instituted claims proceedings against the South Eastern Railway Company who were the carriers responsible for the safe transportation of the gold bullion from London to Paris.

The British authorities insisted that the security measures in place were such that it was impossible for the bullion to have been stolen between London and Boulogne, whilst the police in France insisted that the theft could not possibly have taken place there.

Extensive police enquiries both in Britain and France revealed no clues whatsoever as to how the bullion was stolen or who the culprits were. It appeared that a large quantity of gold bullion had just disappeared into thin air. Police, railway and bank officials were completely baffled by the events which had taken place and they would have to come to terms with the fact that the criminals responsible would never be apprehended.

After all the publicity of the great gold bullion robbery had died down, William Pierce fulfilled a lifelong ambition of becoming a turf accountant after purchasing a betting shop in central London. He told his friends and family that he was able to do so after winning a considerable amount of money on the horses. James Burgess continued working as a train guard whilst investing money in foreign finance bonds as well as buying shares in a London brewery. William Tester continued working for the South Eastern Railway for several more months before leaving the company to work as a manager for a railway company in Sweden. He also invested heavily in foreign finance bonds.

There is no doubt that the master criminal who meticulously planned this audacious crime was Edward Agar, a professional career criminal who could quite easily pass himself off as a gentleman. He was a middle-aged man who had made his fortune. He was now in a position to settle down, put his criminal past behind him and live the rest of his life as an affluent Victorian gentleman. For some reason, he decided not to do that. He did not want a life of luxury but preferred to continue seeking the thrills and excitement of a life of crime, the life he had always known. Sadly for him, it would result in his downfall.

Less than six months after his success with the gold bullion raid, Agar could not resist an opportunity to participate in a swindle which would net him £700 in hard cash (almost £80,000 today) by tendering a forged cheque. Unfortunately for Agar, lady luck was not on his side and he was apprehended by police. Agar subsequently appeared before the Central Criminal Court (Old Bailey) in London to face charges of forgery and uttering. He pleaded not guilty to the charges but was found guilty by the jury. After hearing the previous convictions of Agar and his life of crime, the Judge sentenced him to transportation for life. Agar was subsequently incarcerated in Newgate Prison in London to await transportation.

At the time of his arrest, Agar was living with a woman, Fanny Kay, and they had a young child. After being sentenced to be transported to a penal colony for life, Agar made arrangements to support his family. He arranged for his solicitor to hand the sum of £3,000 (over £340,000 today) to William Pierce, his partner in crime on the bullion robbery, with instructions on how the money should be invested and the sum of money which was to be paid monthly to support Fanny and their child. Pierce agreed to ensure that they would be well cared for. Pierce made regular payments to Fanny for a number of months, then for some reason, decided to double-cross Agar and keep the money for himself. The payments to Fanny came to an abrupt halt which seemed to confirm the old saying; 'there is no honour amongst thieves'.

In the summer of 1856, Fanny Kay, with no income whatsoever and no money with which to buy food for herself and her young child, visited

Newgate Prison out of desperation where she spoke to the prison governor. She told him of her plight and begged for help. She informed the governor that in return, she could supply him with information about the persons responsible for the South Eastern Railway bullion raid, before giving him the names of the people involved.

In October 1856, Agar, who was still being held in prison awaiting transportation, was interviewed by police on several occasions but refused to say anything about the bullion raid. He remained silent for several weeks, despite repeated attempts by police for information. Eventually, realising that Agar would never divulge the information they wanted, the police offered him a deal in which Agar himself would not face charges in relation to the bullion raid, provided he turned Queen's evidence and testified against his accomplices. He was further informed that although his sentence for transportation could not be rescinded or commuted, if he were to testify, favourable consideration would be given for him to receive an early pardon to avoid him being transported for life. After serious consideration and in view of him being double-crossed by Pierce who had stolen the money intended to support his family, he agreed to testify and gave a full written statement about the bullion raid to police.

William Pierce and James Burgess were later arrested. Police were unable to arrest William Tester as he was living in Sweden. Tester was however informed that he was wanted by the British Police for questioning in connection with the bullion raid and subsequently dismissed from the employ of the Swedish Railway Company. Tester then decided that as there was no longer a future for him in Sweden, rather than remain a fugitive for the rest of his life, he may as well return to Britain and face the music. Upon his return to Britain, he surrendered himself to the police authorities.

On Tuesday, 13 January 1857, William Pierce, aged 40, James Burgess, aged 35 and William Tester, aged 26, appeared before Judge Baron Martin at the Central Criminal Court in London charged with stealing the gold bullion. Pierce, who was not employed by the South Eastern Railway Company at that time, having been dismissed earlier for misconduct, faced one charge of simple larceny. Burgess and Tester, who at the time of the offence were both employed by the South Eastern Railway Company, were charged with the more serious offence of larceny servant, i.e. stealing from their employer. The three men pleaded not guilty. Agar testified against his former partners in crime, outlining in detail the part played by each of the defendants in committing the crime. When questioned under oath, Agar admitted to being a professional criminal for the whole of his adult life. Barristers acting on behalf of the three accused, each addressed the jury, stating that they should not believe a man such as Agar who has admitted devoting his whole life to that of crime. The jury did however believe what Agar had told them and when asked by the judge to retire and consider their verdict, they took just ten minutes to return a guilty verdict against each of the defendants. Judge Martin said of Edward Agar, 'He is a man who is as bad as a man can be, but he is a man of the most extraordinary ability. No person who heard him being examined in this court can deny that.' One newspaper journalist reported Judge Martin as having a 'grudging admiration' for Agar.

James Burgess and William Tester were each sentenced to fourteen years transportation and were conveyed by a convict ship to the Swan River Penal Colony in Western Australia in August 1858. William Pierce was given a more lenient sentence due to the fact that he was not an employee of the South Eastern Railway Company at the time of the offence. He received two years penal servitude, of which three months was spent in solitary confinement.

Edward Agar was eventually transported to Australia in September 1857 to serve his original sentence for forgery and uttering. He was imprisoned in a penal colony but did receive his early pardon for turning Queen's evidence in the gold bullion trial as promised. He was released from the penal colony in September 1860, just five years after his conviction for forgery, when he was given a 'ticket of leave' (parole), before receiving his conditional pardon in 1867.

Chapter 3

Murder and Violence

Railway Detective Stabbed to Death

Perhaps the most infamous murder of a railway policeman whilst on duty during the nineteenth century was that involving Detective Sergeant Robert Kidd. The incident in question occurred at Wigan on the evening of Sunday, 29 September 1895 when Detective Sergeant Robert Kidd of the London and North Western Railway Police was attacked and stabbed to death after disturbing a gang of intruders who were stealing confectionery from goods wagons stabled at Chapel Lane Railway Sidings in Wigan.

The circumstances surrounding this case are that Detective Sergeant Kidd, together with Detective Constable Osbourne had arranged to keep evening and night observations on some wagons, due to them being persistently targeted by thieves whilst stabled overnight in the railway sidings. The two officers arrived at the sidings on foot, just after dark at about eight o'clock in the evening and upon entering the sidings they disturbed some intruders who were already raiding the covered wagons. Both officers apprehended different members of the gang who put up fierce resistance. In a frenzied attack, one of the gang members pulled out a knife and stabbed Sergeant Kidd nine times to the face, neck and chest before making good his escape. Sergeant Kidd collapsed in a pool of blood.

In the meantime, Detective Constable Osbourne was attacked and badly beaten by two other gang members, and although he managed to strike one of his assailants a number of times with his truncheon, another gang member intervened until Osbourne was left badly beaten and collapsed on the ground in a state of exhaustion.

All the gang members then ran away. Detective Osbourne managed to get to his feet and went to the assistance of Sergeant Kidd who managed to speak a few words before lapsing into unconsciousness. Osbourne attempted to carry Kidd but after about ten yards he placed him under a wagon and went to summon assistance. Sergeant Kidd later died whilst still under the wagon. Osbourne did manage to reach a signal box and raise the alarm before he too lapsed into unconsciousness. He was conveyed to hospital and fortunately, he did eventually make a full recovery from his injuries.

Meanwhile, an immediate investigation was carried out by three separate police forces. The scene of the crime was on the border between the jurisdiction of the Wigan Borough Constabulary and the Lancashire County Constabulary. The first senior police officer on the scene was Superintendent MacIntosh, who in the absence of Chief Constable Captain Bell was in overall command of the Wigan Borough Constabulary. He mustered as many available officers as possible and started immediate enquiries at the homes of well-known local thieves and other possible suspects.

Superintendent Brassington of the Lancashire County Police also attended the scene with a large detachment of officers from his Constabulary and although he arrived after it had been established that the railway sidings were within the Borough of Wigan, it was decided that as he was already in attendance, his officers would be deployed to assist in the initial stages of the investigation.

The other police force to have jurisdiction at the crime scene was the London and North Western Railway Police force who had foremost authority regarding jurisdiction. Detectives Davern and Buckingham of the LNWR Police were quickly on the scene and Detective Superintendent Elijah Copping from the LNWR Police headquarters in London was informed and he arrived later to take charge of the investigation.

In the meantime, officers of the Wigan Borough Police, under the command of Superintendent MacIntosh had achieved some initial success with their house-to-house enquiries and a total of five men were arrested on suspicion of being involved. The men were all residents of Kay's Houses, a cluster of cottages backing on to the railway sidings where the murder had taken place. Each of the men were coal miners working at local collieries. The five men were subsequently charged with being concerned in the wilful murder of Robert Kidd. Over the next three days, three other men were also arrested in connection with the incident.

This case culminated with three men appearing before Mr Justice Henn Collins at Liverpool Assizes on 26 November 1895. Elijah Winstanley aged 31 and William Kearsley aged 43 were both charged with the wilful murder

A quantity of solid silver ingots, similar to those stolen from the Midland Railway Company during a daring broad daylight raid in Central London in September 1895 (p. 24-26).

This picture gives an indication of the vast quantities of coal which was being transported on the British railway network during the nineteenth and early twentieth century.

At a time when coal fuelled the nation, millions of tons of coal could be found all over the railway network in coal wagons and stockpiled on the ground. Vast amounts of coal were used in the railway industry alone to fuel the many thousands of steam locomotives as well as provide heating for all manner of railway buildings, ranging from office blocks to signal boxes, works, depots, hotels and even station waiting rooms. It was also used to fuel the fleets of steamships and ferries owned and operated by the numerous railway companies. Some railway companies such as the Taff Vale Railway, who made their fortunes transporting large quantities of coal dubbed the mineral 'black diamonds' (p.26-27).

A typical Victorian railway warehouse built for the storage of goods. These massive buildings were vulnerable to being targeted by thieves. Electronic security alarm systems and other sophisticated devices had not been invented during in the nineteenth century (p.53).

A quantity of lead shot used in the manufacture of shotgun cartridges. This type of shot was used to replace the gold stolen in the First Great Train Robbery (p.53-62).

Right: Photograph of Detective Sergeant Robert Kidd of the London and North Western Railway Police, brutally murdered at Wigan in September (p.63-65).

Below: Plaque displayed at Wigan Railway Station, commemorating Detective Sergeant Robert Kidd, murdered whilst on duty in September 1895 (p.66).

Above left and above right: Depiction of the execution of Louise Massett at Newgate prison in January 1900 (p.71-74).

Below: Paddington Station in the 1850s (p.74-76).

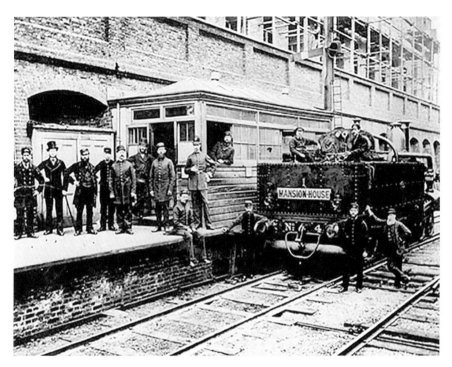

In 1880, like most other railway companies, the Metropolitan Railway had its own railway police force who worked closely with other Metropolitan Railway staff members, including station porters and ticket collectors like those who went to the assistance of Clarence Lewis and detained his assailant until the arrival of the Railway Police. Pictured below is a photograph, believed to have been taken in 1876, just four years before the incident, showing a Railway Policeman with staff members employed by the Metropolitan District Railway (p.92-95).

Valentine Baker. A former disgraced British Army officer who was bestowed the title Lieutenant General Baker Pasha of the Turkish Ottoman army when this photograph was taken circa 1877 (p.95-100).

Left: George Hudson. 'The Railway King' (1800-1871) (p.108-111).

Below: A nineteenth century public awareness notice, informing train passengers to be on their guard against pickpockets whilst travelling on the railway (p.118-122).

A Stephenson six-wheeled coupled engine introduced onto the Taff Vale
Railway in August 1846 to work passenger train services between Cardiff and
Merthyr Tydfil. The locomotive bears the name *Newbridge,* a town located on
the TVR between Merthyr and Cardiff. The town was renamed Pontypridd in
1856.

   This was the type of locomotive (and may have been the actual locomotive)
which was derailed near Merthyr Tydfil in 1847, after two lengths of railway
line were removed by William Scott (p.128-130). This very early photograph
was taken at Cardiff C.1850. (*Viv Head – BTP History Group*)

Depiction of the South Eastern Railway fatal accident involving a Folkestone to London passenger boat train whilst crossing the Beult viaduct at Staplehurst in Kent on 9 June 1865 (p.138-141).

of Robert Kidd. A third defendant, William Halliwell aged 31 was charged with feloniously wounding William Henry Osbourne. The three men pleaded not guilty. Judge Collins instructed that Halliwell be removed from the dock in order for him to be called as a witness to give Queen's evidence against the other two in the principal trial of wilful murder.

At the conclusion of the trial, the jury deliberated for a mere ten minutes before returning a guilty verdict against Winstanley and Kearsley on the capital charge of the wilful murder of Robert Kidd. They were both sentenced to death by hanging. On the direction of the judge, no evidence was offered against William Halliwell who had turned Queen's evidence at the trial. He was discharged.

After the two men had been found guilty, Elijah Winstanley declared that he himself had stabbed Kidd to death and that Kearsley was not involved in the actual stabbing.

In view of this statement, the death sentence imposed on William Kearsley was later commuted to that of life imprisonment. A letter was sent from the Home Secretary to James Wilson, the solicitor acting for Kearsley, stipulating that the sentence imposed upon his client would be further considered after the prisoner had completed a minimum of ten years penal servitude, although no pledge could be given as to the result.

William Kearsley served his penal servitude at Dartmoor Prison. He did not serve the minimum period of ten years as instructed by the Home Secretary. He was released from Dartmoor in February 1903, after serving seven years and three months. Upon his release, he returned home to his wife and family in Wigan.

Elijah Winstanley was hanged at Walton Prison, Liverpool on 17 December 1895. His body was later buried within the precincts of the prison. The executioner was James Billington from Bolton in Lancashire.

The victim in this tragic case was Detective Sergeant Robert Kidd, age thirty-seven. Robert Kidd had originally served as a constable in the Manchester City Police Force, before leaving to join the London and North Western Railway Police in 1885. He performed duties as a uniformed constable before being appointed detective constable at Warrington in 1887. He transferred to Liverpool Edge Hill Station the following year, before being promoted to detective sergeant at Manchester in 1889, where he continued to serve until the day of his death. On that fateful day, he had travelled from Manchester to Wigan by train to assist Detective Constable Osbourne. At the time of his death, he was living at 17, Zebra Street, Salford with his wife Ellen, and their seven children, all under the age of twelve.

In 2021, the British Transport Police History Group (BTPHG) arranged for a blue plaque to be unveiled at Wigan North Western Railway Station, to commemorate the 126th anniversary of the murder of Detective Sergeant Robert Kidd.

The event was attended by a number of retired British Transport Police officers, as well as serving officers, railway staff and members of Robert Kidd's family. A commemoration service was conducted by Philip Bawn the BT Police Force chaplain, who later performed a short service of remembrance at Salford cemetery where the former officer is buried. After the service, a wreath was laid on his grave, on behalf of the BTPHG.

Signalman Molested a Lady Passenger

On Saturday, 23 February 1878, Margaret Owen, a 27 year old housewife, went to Aber Railway Station near Llanfairfechan in North Wales where she had been staying with her in-laws whilst recovering from an illness. Her in-laws resided in the village. She was accompanied to the station by her father-in law and brother-in-law, arriving there at about 7.40pm to catch a train back to her home in Holyhead.

Upon arrival at the station, Mrs Owen went to the booking office and asked for a ticket to Holyhead. The booking clerk issued the ticket and handed it to a man standing alongside him inside the booking office. The man then gave the ticket to Mrs Owen. After buying her ticket, Mrs Owen went to the waiting room on the station platform to await her train. The man who had handed the ticket to Mrs Owen was 24-year-old John Prytherch, a signalman on the station, employed by the London and North Western Railway Company. He had just finished work and about to travel home to Bangor on the same train as the one Mrs Owen was waiting for.

Whilst Mrs Owen was sitting in the waiting room, John Prytherch entered and asked her if she was going to Holyhead, to which she replied 'Yes'. He introduced himself as John Prytherch and asked if she lived in Holyhead to which she replied 'yes'. He went on to say that in the past, he had been living at the Blue Bell public house in Holyhead which was owned by some family relatives. Mrs Owen said that she knew the Prytherch family who lived there.

A few minutes later the Holyhead train arrived at Aber station. Prytherch left the waiting room and went onto the platform followed by Mrs Owen. Prytherch then opened the door of a second class compartment and invited Mrs Owen to climb in which she did. Mrs Owen sat next to the window facing forwards, whilst Prytherch entered the compartment and sat opposite her. There were no other occupants in the compartment.

Shortly after the train departed, Prytherch leaned forward and took hold of Mrs Owens arm, but she pulled it away. He then took hold of her hand and rubbed her wedding ring asking if she was engaged. Mrs Owen told Prytherch that she was married and her husband was meeting the train at Holyhead. Prytherch then became more violent, pulled Mrs Owen towards him and started kissing her.

Mrs Owen then called him a beast and fought off his advances but he pulled her onto the carriage floor. She began to scream. Prytherch then placed his hand up her skirt as she continued to scream and fight him off. Fortunately for Mrs Owen, the train then began to slow down as it approached Bangor Station and Prytherch stopped the assault and sat back down on his seat. He alighted from the train at Bangor which was his destination and he quickly left the station.

Mrs Owen also got off the train at Bangor and reported the matter to the platform inspector William Roberts. The guard of the train was summoned and he placed Mrs Owen in another compartment which contained some ladies, to enable her to continue her journey to Holyhead in safety. When the train arrived at Llanfair, the ladies alighted so the train guard moved Mrs Owen to another carriage under the protection of a local church minister, the Reverend Edwards Roberts, who was also travelling to Holyhead.

Upon arrival at Holyhead, Mrs Owen was met by her husband Rees Owen and her mother. She was upset and in tears as she informed them about the assault committed against her while on the train. The matter was reported to the railway police at Holyhead and Mrs Owen was seen by Detective Howells and a local doctor who examined her. Although no rape had actually taken place, the doctors examination revealed bruising to her arm and her left breast. Her dress was also torn so it was handed to Detective Howells to be retained as evidence.

John Prytherch was later interviewed by police and charged with attempting to ravish Margaret Owen (attempted rape) and an alternative offence of indecent assault. He was subsequently committed by magistrates to stand trial and on Tuesday, 19 March 1879, he appeared before Mr Justice Mellor at the Caernarvonshire Assizes where he pleaded not guilty to both charges. Evidence was presented and upon conclusion of the case, the jury took just five minutes to find the defendant not guilty of attempting to ravish, but guilty of indecent assault.

Mr Justice Mellor informed the jury that although he agreed with their verdict, the maximum sentence which he was allowed to impose for indecent assault was two years imprisonment, which he considered to be far too lenient in this particular case, given the circumstances of the offence and the fact that the prisoner was a trusted railway employee whose duty it was to protect vulnerable female passengers travelling alone, particularly during the evening and night time.

He then sentenced Prytherch to the maximum two years imprisonment with hard labour. Prytherch was also dismissed from the employment of the London and North Western Railway Company who had instigated the court proceedings against him.

The First Railway Murder

It is well documented that the first ever railway murder in Britain took place on the North London Railway between Fenchurch Street and Hackney when Thomas Briggs was murdered by Franz Muller on 9 July 1864. This however is not the case. Whilst Thomas Briggs may well have been the first railway passenger to be murdered whilst travelling by train, the first murder to be committed upon the railway, occurred almost twenty-five years earlier.

The circumstances of this affair go back to December 1840, when John Green started working as a construction superintendent on the Edinburgh to Glasgow Railway, which was in the final stages of construction. Green had previously been in charge of a number of labouring gangs, known as butty gangs, each consisting of about twelve labourers, commonly referred to as navvies (navigators) who had originally built the canal network in Britain and were now involved in the building of railways. Green was an experienced superintendent, used to dealing with navvies and had a reputation of being a rather strict man and a hard taskmaster.

Green started working for the Edinburgh and Glasgow Railway Company on 9 December 1840 at Crosshill, near Bishopsbridge, approximately three miles outside Glasgow. He was placed in charge of a number of butty gangs, the large majority of whom were Irish. On his very first day, he experienced intimidation from a number of workers and was subject to stones and other objects being thrown at him.

The following day, he arrived at the site shortly before seven o'clock in the morning. It was a cold damp day and still quite dark. As he entered the site, he saw a large number of workmen standing in a group. He walked towards them and the majority began to disperse as if going to start work but a small group stayed behind. Green walked past the men and whilst his back was turned, he was hit over the head by one of the men with an iron bar. He slumped to the ground. Another man started to jump up and down on him, whilst the man with the iron bar continued to strike him about the head and body. The attack, which was completely unprovoked was witnessed by a number of people. Both men then fled the scene. Green died less than an hour later.

A local Sheriff Principal (Scottish judicial administrator) later visited the site, in company with a number of soldiers from the 58th Foot Regiment and a total of twenty-three Irish navvies were arrested and taken into custody. The two men who had fled the scene were later named as Dennis Doolan, aged 29, a native of King's County (later re-named County Offaly) and Patrick Redding, aged 25, a native of Tipperary. Their details were circulated as wanted for questioning in connection with the murder of John Green.

Patrick Redding was later arrested in England and escorted back to Glasgow. Dennis Doolan evaded the authorities for almost three weeks before being arrested in Liverpool whilst trying to make his way to America. When arrested, Doolan gave his name as Dennis Hyde, but police were not convinced and they escorted him from Liverpool to Glasgow by steamship. Upon his return to Glasgow his identity was confirmed as Dennis Doolan and he was remanded in custody at Glasgow Prison.

A case against Doolan and Redding was established, which concluded that the murder had been premeditated in order for the labourers to rid themselves of a new superintendent who had a reputation for being a strict, hard taskmaster and who had been put in charge of them. Both men were charged with the wilful murder of John Green.

A third man arrested shortly after the murder had taken place was James Hickie from County Carlow. He was also charged with the wilful murder of Green after it was ascertained that he had obtained the iron bar from a smithy at the railway site and handed it to Redding for use as the murder weapon.

Three other men, John Campbell, Patrick Cosgrove and George Cox were also charged in connection with the murder.

The murder trial took place at the Circuit Court in Glasgow on 22 March 1841. Three of the defendants, Campbell, Cosgrove and Cox, turned Queen's Evidence and gave their evidence on oath, taking care not to implicate themselves. The other three defendants pleaded not guilty to the charge of wilful murder. An overwhelming mass of evidence was produced by the prosecution. Consequently, no evidence was offered by the defence, who accepted the principal facts, but the three defendants blamed each other for the murder.

After a hearing which had lasted for twelve hours, it took the jury just forty-five minutes to find Dennis Doolan, Patrick Redding (both unanimous verdicts) and James Hickie (majority verdict), guilty of the wilful murder of John Green. A unanimous recommendation of mercy was made by the jury in respect of the defendant Hickie who had taken no active part in the actual assault on Green which led to his death.

All three men were sentenced to death by hanging, the sentence of which (upon the direction of the judge), was to be carried out near the scene of the murder, alongside the railway line at Crosshill. The three men were transported to Glasgow Prison to await execution. The sentence against Hickie was later commuted to transportation for life, and the execution of Doolan and Redding was set to take place on 14 May 1841.

On Thursday 13 May 1841, scaffolding from Glasgow prison was transported to the execution site where the gallows was erected. Soldiers remained at the site until the following day as a security precaution.

That evening at Glasgow prison, Bishop Murdock (a Roman Catholic Bishop) remained with Doolan and Redding until ten o'clock before leaving the cell. After he left, three laymen remained with the prisoners for the rest of the night, although neither of the prisoners slept. The next morning, they were escorted from their cell to the front of the prison and placed into a large open carriage. Both wore handcuffs and were manacled together by chains fitted to their legs.

At eight o'clock, a procession left Glasgow prison for Crosshill. It was headed by cavalry on horseback, followed by the large open carriage in which the two condemned men were elevated so they could be seen by spectators as the procession passed by. Bishop Murdock with an assistant was also in the carriage. More cavalry travelled behind the carriage, followed by over 600 infantry and two troops of Dragoon Guards. Either side of the procession were flanked by police. The procession reached its destination at a quarter to ten and after a short time in religious devotion with Bishop Murdock, both men confessed to the murder of John Green and begged his forgiveness. They both insisted that they had never intended to murder Green when they planned the attack, but they did intend to give him a sound beating.

The executions were carried out at precisely ten o'clock. Both bodies were later placed in coffins and transported to Glasgow Prison where they were interred within the precincts of the prison that same evening. The mass of the local population, estimated to be in excess of 100,000 people turned out to watch the public execution, the biggest turn out that had ever been seen in the city or in the vicinity of Glasgow. Everything passed over without the slightest incident and there was not the slightest sign of a riot, which had been feared by some.

French Governess Hanged for Murder

Louise Masset, a French Governess, lived in Stoke Newington, London with her married sister. Louise was not married but in 1896, at the age of 29, she gave birth to an illegitimate child, a baby boy who was christened Manfred Masset. The boy's father, a wealthy Frenchman who lived in France financially supported his son by sending money to Louise on a regular basis. When Manfred attained the age of three, his mother placed him in the care of a nanny, Miss Gentle, who raised the boy at her home in Tottenham, London. Louise visited her son regularly and paid Miss Gentle for his keep.

In October 1899, Louise informed Miss Gentle that Manfred's father was taking custody of the boy to raise and educate him in France and arrangements were made for Miss Gentle to take Manfred to London Bridge railway station to be handed over to Louise. These arrangements were later altered and Miss Gentle was told to hand over the boy to Louise outside a public house at Stamford Hill. At about 12.45pm on the 27 October, Manfred was handed over to his mother by Miss Gentle as arranged.

After collecting the child, Louise and the boy travelled by bus from Stamford Hill to London Bridge railway station, arriving about an hour later. They entered the railway station and went into a waiting room, where Louise informed the attendant that she had arranged to meet someone there. Louise and the boy remained in the waiting room until approximately

2.45pm when they left. Louise informed the waiting room attendant that they were going to the refreshment room. The attendant did not see the boy again, but she did see Louise, alone, washing her hands in the ladies' toilet just after 7pm that evening.

Just half an hour earlier however, the naked body of Manfred had been found wrapped in a black shawl in the ladies toilet at Dalston Junction railway station in East London. Examination of the body showed that death had been caused by suffocation, but a serious injury had also been inflicted by a blow from an object to the head, either just before, or immediately after death. Lying beside the body was a clinker brick, which was believed to be the object used to deliver the blow.

Police enquiries later revealed that the brick was almost identical to other bricks which formed a rock garden at the home of Louise Masset in Stoke Newington.

Louise Masset did not go home that evening, but caught the 7.22pm train from London Bridge to Brighton. The following afternoon, a brown paper parcel was found in the waiting room at Brighton railway station. The parcel was found to contain clothing of a child, from which labels and trimmings had been removed, presumably in an attempt to prevent identification. The clothes in question were later shown to Miss Gentle, who by means of a particular tear and a grease mark, was able to identify the clothes as those worn by Manfred Masset on the day his body was found. Miss Gentle also identified the body found at Dalston Junction station, as being that of Manfred Masset.

Further enquiries into the death of Manfred revealed that Louise had purchased a black shawl from a shop in Stoke Newington just three days before to the body was found and the shawl appeared to be identical to the one wrapped around the body of the child when it was discovered.

On the morning of Monday, 30 October 1899, Police visited the home of Louise Masset in Stoke Newington, only to find that she had left the house earlier that morning and again gone to Brighton. In a statement later, she said that she had read of the murder of her son in a newspaper and in a panic had gone to visit her brother-in-law in Brighton. She is alleged to have told him, 'I am wanted for murder, but I have not done it'. She was advised by her brother-in-law to go to the police but stated that she was afraid to do so. The following day, Louise Masset was arrested by police in Croydon.

After her arrest, Louise Masset protested her innocence but agreed to take part in an identification parade where she was picked out by the attendant who saw her leave the waiting room at London Bridge Station with the boy on the afternoon in question. She also saw her return alone about 7pm, just half an hour after the body of Manfred had been discovered.

Louise told the police that the reason she went to London Bridge station was to hand the boy over to two women who had offered to take care of him for an annual payment of twelve pounds. She was unable to identify either of the two women. She denied telling Miss Gentle that Manfred going to live in France with his father. Louise was subsequently charged with the wilful murder of her son Manfred, to which she replied, 'Impossible.'

A coroner's inquest was held at Hackney on 16 November 1899, when the jury returned a verdict of unlawful killing of Manfred by his mother Louise. She was committed to stand trial at the Central Criminal Court, London, on a Coroner's Warrant.

The trial of Louise Masset took place at the Central Criminal Court (Old Bailey) on Monday, 18 December 1899. Mr Justice Bruce presided. Lord Coleridge represented the defendant who pleaded 'not guilty' to a charge of wilful murder.

After the prosecution case was presented, Lord Coleridge emphasised that no witnesses had seen Louise Masset at Dalston Junction railway station on the day of the murder and suggested that it was possible that one of the two women described but not named by Masset had committed the crime before going to Brighton, knowing that Louise Masset was going there. That person could then have left the parcel of clothing at Brighton station in order to incriminate Louise.

The jury however did not accept this version of events and after deliberating for just twenty-five minutes found Masset guilty of the wilful murder of her son Manfred. She was sentenced to death by hanging. After the verdict was announced, Judge Bruce asked Masset if she had anything to say. She continued to protest her innocence. Throughout the trial, Louise Masset had exhibited the utmost composure but when the judge assumed the black cap, she broke down and at the conclusion of the proceedings was in such a state of collapse that she had to be assisted from the dock by two female warders.

After her conviction was announced, Louise continued to protest her innocence and a petition on her behalf was organised by the French governesses in London, together with a number of local residents. The petition was even sent to Queen Victoria. The petition was to no avail and the law took its course. The sentence was carried out and Louise confessed to the murder of her son just before she was hanged at Newgate prison in London on 9 January 1900.

Gruesome Discovery on the Great Western Railway

On Sunday 29 October 1848, Mr Watson, a passenger from Exeter was on Slough railway station when he saw a pine box unattended on the station platform. He drew the matter to the attention of a railway porter. The box did not appear to belong to any of the passengers on the station, so the porter treated it as lost property. The box remained at Slough railway station for a number of weeks without being claimed. The lost property regulations on the Great Western Railway at the time stipulated that any lost property found anywhere upon the railway and subsequently unclaimed, must be forwarded to the main lost property at Paddington Station where it would be held for a minimum of twelve months before being disposed of by public auction. In consequence, the box was forwarded to the Paddington lost property office.

The procedure adopted at Paddington in relation to lost property forwarded to them, was that a full examination of all lost property which had been on hand for over twelve months would be carried out on an annual basis. Only after that inspection and if the owner could not be traced was property to be sold by public auction. As a result of these procedures, the pine box remained in the Lost Property Office at Paddington for some nineteen months after it had been found, before being closely inspected with a view to its disposal.

On Saturday, 1 June 1850, the box was opened by Mr Bailey, the person in overall charge of the lost property department. He made a gruesome discovery. To his horror, he found the mutilated body of what appeared to be a young child wrapped in a piece of calico. Mr Bailey immediately reported the matter to Mr Seymour, General Manager of the Great Western Railway, who in turn contacted Superintendent Collard, Chief of the Great Western Railway Police who started an immediate investigation.

On Tuesday, 4 June 1850, an inquest was held at the Lord Hill Public House at North Wharf Road, Paddington. The Inquest was presided over by the Middlesex (Western Division) Coroner, Mr Wakley. The matter was subject of a report in the *Newcastle Guardian & Tyne Mercury*, 8 June 1850 which reads as follows;

MURDERED – On Tuesday, Mr Wakeley held an inquest at the Lord Hill, Public House, Paddington on the body of a child about 18 months old, which was discovered on the Great Western Railway on 29th October 1848 in a deal box, about 14 inches square and 10 ½ inches deep, sewed up in a piece of canvas. Mr Watson, a passenger from Exeter, found it on the platform of Slough station and handed it to one of the porters. As no one claimed it, it was brought up to London and placed in the lost property department. It was there until last Saturday 1 June, that being the annual day when lost property is examined.

Mr Bailey, the superintendent of that department, opened the box, and discovered the body of the deceased, which was carefully folded up in a piece of calico. It had all the appearance of a mummy, having been evidently pressed down in the box. A cambric handkerchief was tied tightly around its throat. There were cuts about the arms and legs, showing that there had been attempts to sever the limbs from the body. Mr Collard, superintendent of police, and Mr Seymour, manager of the company have been attempting to discover the perpetrator of the murder, but without effect. Doctor Thorn, surgeon, Harrow Road, said that the body was covered with flannel clothing. There were four teeth in the upper and two teeth in the lower jaws. Over the shoulder joint of the right arm he found two deep cuts close together, showing that a blundering had been made to remove the arm at the socket by someone unacquainted with anatomical principles. The left arm and both thighs had been cut in a similar manner. He was of the opinion that the child was from 15 to 18 months old. He had not the least doubt that the death was the result of strangulation. Verdict; Wilful murder against some person or persons unknown, The coroner directed Mr Collard not to relax his exertions in order to discover the guilty parties, which he promised to do.

An extract from the *Windsor & Eton Express*. 8 June 1850 added, 'The body was so horribly mutilated that its sex could not be discovered. The sexual structure was completely removed'.

Superintendent Collard did continue to investigate the murder but he had little or no chance of ever solving the case. At that time, forensic science was unheard of. Basic blood grouping techniques would not be discovered for over half a century and fingerprint evidence was not successfully used in British courts until 1902. Furthermore, it could not be established whether the victim was a boy or a girl and the murder had been committed more than eighteen months before the remains of the body were discovered inside the box.

Due to the case remaining unsolved, it was never possible to ascertain where the murder actually took place. If the murder did take place upon the railway, it would have been the second railway murder ever to have been committed in Britain, although it is highly likely that the murder was committed elsewhere before the body was brought onto the railway and left either accidentally or intentionally at Slough Station for some unknown reason. In any event this was a very gruesome murder of a very young child, the circumstances of which will forever remain a mystery.

Other Gruesome Railway Packages

In December 1843, a parcel was transported from London to Winchester by the South Western Railway Company. The parcel was addressed to Mr Muspratt, an ironmonger in the city. When the railway company attempted to deliver the parcel, it was discovered that the ironmonger's shop was no longer owned by Mr Muspratt, who had recently died. The parcel was endorsed as 'undelivered' and returned to Winchester station with a view to being returned to the sender. Sometime later, in an attempt to locate the person who sent the parcel, it was opened by a railway constable who made a very unpleasant discovery. Inside the parcel was a wicker basket which contained a white calico bag wrapped in paper and tied at the neck by a piece of white tape. This bag was strongly scented with musk. Inside this bag, the constable found another bag made of white oilskin, also tied at the neck with tape. Upon opening it, he saw what appeared to be the body of a newly-born male child. It did not appear to be decomposed and there were no visible signs of external violence. Superintendent Dalby of the South Western Railway Police was summoned and the matter became the subject of a murder investigation.

An inquest was held later that afternoon before Mr J.W. Todd, the Winchester Coroner, who adjourned the inquest pending further enquiries by Superintendent Dalby. On 22 January 1844 the inquest resumed at the White Swan public house in Winchester.

Mr Smith, a surgeon, told the inquest that he had carried out a post mortem examination of the body. He stated that the lungs floated in water, which he considered clearly proved that the child was born alive. There were some slight abrasions on the arms, which the surgeon imagined had been caused whilst packing up the child whilst still alive. The head was the most decomposed part of the body, which led him to believe that it may have been injured wilfully, although after considering all the circumstances, he could not determine whether any violence had in fact been used, or whether the infant died through neglect on the part of its parents.

Superintendent Dalby told the inquest that he had made extensive enquiries and ascertained that the basket in which the child was sent had been bought at a shop in Oxford Street, London, but the proprietor, Mr Cuttings, was unable to supply details as to who bought it. Superintendent Dalby stated that the package did not contain any information as to who had sent it and subsequent enquiries made by him were to no avail.

The Coroner decided that there was little point in continuing with any further enquiries to discover the guilty party as it was very probable that the person concerned, would never be discovered. The jury subsequently returned an open verdict after deciding that although it was confirmed that the child's body had been sent from London to Winchester by train, there was no evidence to show by whom it was sent, or by what means it came to its death. The case remained unsolved.

Less than three years later, in November 1846, a similar incident occurred when yet another package containing the body of a child was sent by train. On 20 November 1846, a parcel was taken to Nottingham railway station by a young woman, to be sent by train to Mr W.J. Smith in Suffolk. The parcel was handed to porter Willoughby, who was on duty in the station parcels office.

The woman told Willoughby that the parcel was fragile and should not be crushed. She stated it should be conveyed with great care and if possible, be put on a seat along with the passengers. There was little else that porter Willoughby could recollect about the woman, other than she was young, short with a dark complexion. The parcel was subsequently despatched by train from Nottingham to London.

Some six days later, on 26 November, the parcel arrived back in Nottingham at half past two in the morning on a night mail train. The parcel was endorsed as undelivered and to be returned to sender. Porter Willoughby, who was again on duty, opened the parcel in an attempt to establish who has sent it. Inside the parcel, to his shock and horror, he found a wicker basket, containing the body of a dead infant. The mouth appeared to have had considerable moisture around it, which had become green and mouldy.

Beneath the body was a quantity of cloths and straw, together with a letter addressed to 'W.J. Smith, Esq; Suffolk.' The hand written letter requested that the father of the infant should take care of it and it warned him against seducing anyone else as he had done to her. The gruesome discovery and letter was immediately handed over to the police and a coroner's jury assembled. The coroner's inquest was immediately adjourned until the following Saturday to allow time for a post mortem examination.

A post mortem on the body was later carried out by Mr W. Yates, a surgeon at the Nottingham Dispensary who concluded that the infant was a fine and well-formed female about a week old. There were no marks of violence upon the body. It was his opinion that the body had been put into the basket alive and had died partially through want of nourishment, partially owing to cold, and partially from the effects of an overdose of opiate.

The inquest was held and was adjourned sine-die by the Coroner for further inquiries to be made by Superintendent Rogerson of the Nottingham Police. It would appear that the young woman who sent the parcel was never traced and no charges were ever brought against any individual in connection with this matter.

A third case, similar to the two aforementioned incidents, occurred in 1842, but on this occasion the person involved, Sarah Drake, was apprehended and dealt with by the judiciary. In this incident, the gruesome package was sent from London to an address in Cheshire.

Sarah Drake was born in 1814 and entered domestic service at a young age. By the time she was in her early twenties she had progressed to become a cook/housekeeper, the most senior servant role in the household.

In 1841 whilst in the service of Mr Catley, a London gentleman residing in Leytonstone, she entered into a relationship with Joseph Timperley, a married man from Cheshire. The relationship resulted in an unwanted pregnancy. In April 1842, Sarah gave birth to a baby boy. She did not mention the birth to anyone but kept the baby in her room at the house where she was employed. Other servants in the house had gossiped about her 'being in the family way' but no particular notice was taken until her physical appearance tended to confirm a belief amongst the servants that she had given birth.

A few days later, Sarah asked one of her fellow servants to lend her a sturdy box, stating that she wanted to send some things to a relative in the country. A small pine box was given to her and she took it into her bedroom. She later emerged from her room and asked another servant for some brown paper, which was given to her. Sarah then wrapped the pine box in the brown paper. The servant who originally gave her the box would later give evidence that the box was much heavier when Sarah brought it out of the room than when she had taken it in. After wrapping the box in brown paper, Sarah asked a footman to write a name and address on the package. She asked him to write; 'Mr Timperley. Knutsford Union Workhouse, Cheshire', which he did. The package was taken to Euston railway station in London where it was forwarded by train to its destination and delivered to the workhouse in Knutsford on 15 April.

When the box was opened, it was found to contain the dead body of a baby boy, wrapped in a shawl and a piece of fine linen, which was covered in dry blood. Also inside the box was a slip of paper upon which was written 'you will do your wife a favour by burying this'. Police were summoned and an inquest was arranged by the Cheshire coroner. The inquest was adjourned pending further enquires.

Sarah Drake was interviewed by police at the home of Mr Catley in Leytonstone. On seeing the police, Sarah became very distressed. She admitted giving birth to the baby, but she stated that the child was stillborn and not knowing what to do with it she sent it to Mr Timperley, the father of the baby. Sarah Drake was subsequently arrested and taken into custody.

The body of the child was examined by Mr Watson Baird, a doctor who resided at Knutsford. He expressed his belief that the child was born alive. It was a fully developed, healthy male child. There were marks of compression on the neck of the child. Up the right side was the mark of a thumb and on the left side, marks of fingers. He expressed his opinion that the death was occasioned by this violent compression which caused strangulation and that the injuries were caused whilst the child was still alive.

Sarah Drake later appeared before Ilford magistrates court in Essex, charged with the wilful murder of her child. The whole facts of the case were produced in evidence and Sarah Drake was committed to stand trial at the Central Criminal Court (Old Bailey) in London on a charge of wilful murder.

Sarah Drake appeared before the Central Criminal Court on 17 May 1842. Upon the directions of the judge, the charge of wilful murder was not proceeded with, but she pleaded guilty to concealing the birth of her dead male child. She was sentenced to six months imprisonment with hard labour.

Just two years later, in December 1844, Sarah Drake's sister Mary Burton received a box which had been delivered to her home. Upon opening the box, she discovered the dead body of a newly born male child. Sarah was questioned at length about this discovery, and although strongly suspected as the person being responsible for sending the body to her sister, she denied the offence and no action was taken against her due to insufficient evidence.

Five years later however, in December 1849, Sarah Drake again appeared before the Central Criminal Court charged with the wilful murder of yet another illegitimate child, her son Louis Drake aged two years, by strangulation. Sarah was represented by an eminent barrister, Mr Collier. A plea of not guilty on the grounds of insanity was entered on her behalf and despite no witnesses being called to give evidence for the defence, she was found not guilty of wilful murder, on the grounds of temporary insanity. Sarah Drake was confined to the notorious Bedlam Lunatic Asylum, during Her Majesty's Pleasure.

After serving less than ten years in the Asylum, Sarah Drake was released. She continued living in London until her death in 1891 at the age of 77 years. Many people at the time thought that Sarah Drake was extremely lucky to have escaped the hangman's noose and she was even dubbed 'the woman who cheated the hangman'.

In the three year period, between 1842 and 1846, three dead infants were known to have been transported in packages on the railway network. The actual number may well have been much higher and the potential numbers for the whole of the Victoria era are frightening. One can only imagine the pain, suffering and anguish that some girls and young women endured as a result of unwanted pregnancies and the shame that followed during those sad times.

Taff Vale Railway Riot – Police Indicted

The Taff Vale Railway originally ran from Cardiff Docks to Merthyr Tydfil in South Wales and was constructed under the direction of the company's principal civil engineer George Bush and completed in two stages. The first section from Cardiff to Navigation House (Abercynon) opened in October 1840 and the second stage from Abercynon to Merthyr Tydfil opened the following year in April 1841.

An assistant to George Bush was an engineer, George Fisher, who was given the title General Superintendent of the Taff Vale Railway Company and based at the Company Offices in Cardiff. He was also given command of the newly created Taff Vale Railway Police Force with the rank of Superintendent. In effect, George Fisher wore two hats, Civil Engineer and Superintendent/ Chief of Police. He continued in this role for many years and although the arrangement was considered by some as being far from satisfactory, it suited the needs and requirements of the TVR company directors.

Police Forces were a new concept in South Wales at that time and little or no precedent had been set for how they should operate. The Glamorgan County Constabulary (in the area where the Taff Vale Railway operated) did not exist when the Taff Vale Railway Police was set up in 1840 but was founded shortly afterwards in 1841.

In 1847, work began on a further expansion of the Taff Vale Railway with the construction of a new branch line from Pontypridd (midway between Cardiff and Merthyr) along the Rhondda Valley to Treherbert, a distance of some ten miles where rich deposits of coal had been found. In 1853, as the new railway line reached just beyond the half-way point, a dispute took place between the Taff Vale Railway Company and another company, Messrs Warren and Denroche, who had been contracted to actually build the branch line to Treherbert. The dispute in question revolved around some property, mainly plant equipment and construction materials, which were on a construction site being used by Messrs Warren and Denroche at a location known as Glyncornel near Llwynypia. The Taff Vale Railway Company maintained that property on the site belonged to them and that the construction company was refusing to hand it over, whilst Mr William Taylor Warren, one of the company directors (Messrs Warren and Denroche), insisted that the property in question had been bought and paid for by his company. The matter was brought to the attention of Superintendent Fisher who took it upon himself to sort the matter out using his authority as the Chief of Police.

The Taff Vale Railway Police at the time consisted of fifty or more officers wearing uniforms. The uniforms consisted of a dark blue tail coat with leather belt and trousers. Cravats and top hats were worn and officers were routinely issued with truncheons, although swords were also available for use where necessary.

When William Warren became aware of the Taff Vale Railway Police involvement in the dispute, he sensed that there may be some partiality, due to the police force being employed by the railway company involved, so he in turn called in the local Glamorgan County Constabulary. Initially, Police Constable Ebenezer Jenkins attended the construction site. He was the local constable and in fact the only constable responsible for the policing the whole of the Rhondda Valley on behalf of the local county force. Police Constable Jenkins immediately informed his senior officer, Police Superintendent Thomas, who was the district officer in charge of the Glamorgan County police, stationed at Pontypridd.

Superintendent Thomas and a number of officers, including PC Jenkins, attended the construction site on 28 November 1853 after receiving information that Superintendent Fisher and his officers from the Taff Vale Railway Police were about to visit the site. As expected, Superintendent Fisher turned up with a number of his officers and they were accompanied by a bunch of railwaymen carrying branding irons and tins of paint. Warren spoke to Superintendent Fisher at the entrance to the site, pointing out that the construction site was private property and if he and his men entered the site they would be trespassing. Superintendent Fisher ignored this and told the railway men to enter the site and mark the disputed property as belonging to the Taff Vale Railway Company.

Superintendent Thomas of the Glamorgan County Constabulary intervened and instructed his officers to form a line in order to prevent Superintendent Fisher's men and the railway workers from entering the site. This course of action was possibly the only occasion in British history when two police forces have come face to face into a potential conflict with each other. The two police superintendents then held a discussion, during which Superintendent Thomas once again requested that Fisher and his men leave the site. This they eventually did, but not before Superintendent Fisher had warned Thomas that he intended to return later with enough men to finish the job.

After Superintendent Fisher and his followers had left the site, Superintendent Thomas instructed PC Jenkins to monitor the situation and keep him posted of all future developments. PC Jenkins complied with the order and during the next few days, he spent most of his time on the construction site but making numerous journeys up and down the valley to and from Pontypridd. PC Jenkins had no form of transport or communication and it is presumed that he made the trips back and forth to Pontypridd (a round trip of about ten miles) on horseback. Whilst he was not provided with a horse by the Constabulary, he would have little trouble in borrowing one from one of the many local farmers in the area.

During the evening and night time, whilst PC Jenkins was off duty, Warren put one of his senior staff members, William Ryan, in charge of security on the site at Glyncornel. A number of men under the direction of Ryan protected the site, most of whom were armed with guns, swords and other weapons. Notices were displayed warning all persons that any horses brought to the site for the purpose of removing property would be immediately shot. It was then decided by William Warren that all the disputed property would be removed from the site altogether in a convoy of wagons and carts. On the 4 December 1853, a large quantity of the disputed property was transported to another site at Llantrisant some nine miles away and arrangements were made for the remaining property to be removed the following day.

News of the removal of property from the site and the proposed convoy due to take the rest of the property the following day quickly reached the ears of Superintendent Fisher who decided to intercept the convoy as it travelled down the valley. On the 5 December 1853, a heavily laden convoy of horse drawn wagons and a carriage containing iron rails left the construction site as planned. It was accompanied by between twenty-five and thirty construction workers led by William Warren and his assistant William Ryan. Police Constable Ebenezer Jenkins was also present as an observer.

As the convoy travelled down the valley through the village of Tonypandy, William Warren and the contractors saw Superintendent Fisher in full uniform, accompanied by a number of other uniformed officers coming up the hill towards them. Superintendent Fisher and some of his men were carrying swords. Immediately behind the officers was a large number of other men, mainly Taff Vale Railway workers, armed with sticks and other weapons. The total numbers estimated in this group was thought to be in the region of 200 men.

As the two groups came together, Superintendent Fisher and his men attacked the contractors; fights broke out and a riot took place. Due to the overwhelming numbers of railwaymen involved, the contractors turned and fled the scene but fighting continued as some of the railwaymen chased and overtook the fleeing contractors. The riot did not last for any great length of time due to the vastly superior numbers of Superintendent Fisher, his officers and their followers.

Fortunately there were no fatalities during the riot, although a number of contractors did sustain lacerations and other injuries during the attack. Perhaps the worst of the casualties was William Ryan who suffered a number of injuries which included stab wounds and lacerations apparently inflicted by a police sword.

A full enquiry into the riot was carried out by the Glamorgan County Constabulary which concluded that whilst the casualty list of the contractors was a long one, there was no evidence of any injuries sustained by the railwaymen, railway police or their followers.

This evidence pointed to them being the aggressors and as such, the leaders, including Superintendent Fisher and the railway policemen (three of whom were armed with swords) were all indicted for to stand trial for riotous behaviour at the next Assizes.

Superintendent Fisher himself was charged with inciting the riot and with feloniously cutting, stabbing and wounding William Ryan with a sword. Thirteen other men charged alongside him were named as follows; Thomas Leyshon, William Gainey, David Morgan, Daniel Driscoll, Richard Phillips, Evan Thomas, Thomas Jacobs, Joseph Davies, William Downes, Edwin Daniels, Jenkin Rees, Rees Jones and Thomas Maunders.

In March 1854, Superintendent George Fisher together with the thirteen other men appeared before the Glamorgan Spring Assizes, which were held in Swansea. The presiding Judge was the Hon. Sir Charles Crompton. The prosecution was conducted by Mr Grove, QC and all the defendants were represented by Mr Gifford QC.

As the trial progressed, evidence was presented that on 13 January 1854 (between the date of the alleged offences on the 5 December 1853 and the present), the Company Messrs Warren and Denroche had gone into liquidation after the company directors William Taylor Warren and Matthew

Denroche had been declared bankrupt at a court hearing in Cardiff. The prosecutor Mr Grove conceded that in view of the company no longer being in existence, establishing lawful ownership of the disputed property could not be achieved. As this was an integral part of the case against the defendants, the ends of justice would best be met by the prisoners entering into their own recognisances to keep the peace for the future and that no evidence would be offered against them. The Judge endorsed this course of action and instructed the jury to find the defendants 'Not Guilty' of all charges. The prisoners were discharged.

It is believed that George Fisher was the first ever police chief in Britain to be indicted to stand trial for a criminal offence and many people considered that Superintendent Fisher and his officers who took part in the riot were lucky not to have faced a full trial and possible conviction. Although their guilt was far from assured and the outcome of such a trial could have gone either way, had they been convicted, they would no doubt have received severe sentences bringing about an abrupt end to their police careers.

George Fisher and his officers did continue their careers with the Taff Vale Railway Police. Fisher himself worked until he retired at the age of 60, after which he continued working for the TVR Company for a number of years, on a part time basis in his capacity of civil engineer. He died at his home in Cardiff in 1891, aged eighty-one.

Was She Pushed Or Did She Jump?

Shortly before midday on Tuesday, 18 January 1853, Mrs Caroline Duffil, age 37, wife of Thomas Duffil, Landlord of the Freemason's Arms public house at Beverley in East Yorkshire travelled by train to nearby Hull. After spending the afternoon in Hull, she caught the last train back which departed Hull at 6.50pm.

After boarding the train, she sat in a third class compartment together with a number of other passengers. The train then proceeded to Cottingham where a number of passengers alighted, leaving Caroline in the compartment with just one other male passenger. The train departed Cottingham for Beverley at 7.02pm and the events which followed are unclear and subject to some conjecture and speculation.

As the train departed from Cottingham station, shouts and screams were heard emanating from the compartment and although it was dark outside, it appeared that someone was either thrown, pushed or jumped from the moving train as it cleared the end of the station platform. Members of staff from the station, walked along the railway line and found Caroline Duffil lying unconscious alongside the railway line. Samuel Watson, a local doctor was summoned and attended the scene before Mrs Duffil was conveyed to the nearby Railway Tavern Hotel. Documents on her person revealed her identity and a messenger visited the Freemason's Arms in Beverley to inform her husband of the incident. Thomas Duffil immediately went to his wife's bedside. Caroline Duffil remained in a coma for six days until, shortly after 8am on Monday, 24 January she died as a result of her injuries.

Returning to the incident itself, after the train in question left Cottingham, it continued its journey to Beverley. As the train slowed down on its approach to the station, a man was seen to jump from the compartment in which Mrs Cottingham had been travelling and run across some fields as he fled the scene.

An investigation ensued and eventually a 31-year-old local dairy farmer, William Holliday, was arrested on suspicion of robbery and attempted murder of Caroline Duffil (Holliday was arrested before Mrs Duffil died of her injuries). William Holliday was conveyed to York Gaol where he was remanded in custody. He was subsequently charged with the manslaughter of Mrs Duffil. The incident was widely reported by members of the press, and the following extracts are taken from newspapers printed at the time:

The *Morning Post*, Tuesday, 25 January 1853

Robbery in a railway carriage and attempted murder.

On Tuesday evening last [18 January 1853] as Mrs Duffil, of Beverley, was returning from Hull to Beverley by the last train, she was, unfortunately left alone in the carriage with a ruffian, who first robbed her and then threw her out of the carriage near Cottingham. It appears that the carriage in which Mrs Duffil was returning home was nearly full of people when the train left Hull, but unfortunately for her, they all got out at Cottingham, except the villain who committed the above atrocious act. It is supposed that, soon after the train had left Cottingham, the fellow had robbed her and in order to get away, threw her out of the carriage as the train was on its way to Beverley. Her cries of 'thief' and 'murder' were heard but when assistance arrived she was insensible and has been so ever since. She is now in a very precarious state. It is thought that the fellow went to Beverley by train, but had jumped out a short distance from the station before it stopped. He is still at large, but strenuous efforts are being made to bring him to justice.

The above newspaper article printed at the time contains certain facts which, in the true traditions of the press, have been grossly exaggerated. Similar article appeared in another newspapers, one of which is set out below:

Newcastle Guardian 29 January 1853

ROBBERY AND MURDER ON A RAILWAY.

In our third page we have given some particulars of a most diabolical affair which took place last week, on the line of railway between Hull and Beverley. In one of the carriages was Mrs Duffil, who had been visiting the former town on business, the only other occupant being a man who is not known. There is no doubt that whilst the train was in motion, the fellow set upon the woman, robbed her and threw her out of the door – to silence her cries and avoid exposure and punishment. Mrs Duffil lingered in a state of insensibility until about 8 o'clock on Monday morning, when she died.

The following article appeared in the *Taunton Courier* on 2 February 1853:

ROBBERY AND ATTEMPTED MURDER IN A
RAILWAY CARRIAGE

One of the most diabolical attempts to murder of which we ever remember was made on Tuesday evening last, at Cottingham, near Hull. The circumstances of this shocking affair are as follows: - Mrs Duffil, the wife of a very highly respectable innkeeper at Beverley, had occasion to visit Hull on Tuesday for the purpose of transacting some business. She left Hull by the last train for Beverley in the evening, taking her seat in a second class carriage. In this carriage were several other persons, who all got out when the train reached Cottingham, with the exception of one man, who was left alone in the carriage with

Mrs Duffil. No sooner was the train in motion again than this fellow set upon the unfortunate woman and robbed her. He threw her out of the carriage, no doubt intending to kill her. The night was dark so the actions of the man could not be seen, but the screams of Mrs Duffil and her cries of 'thief' were heard at the Cottingham station.

The persons who heard these exclamations immediately proceeded up the line, and found the poor woman lying on the line in an insensible state. She was cut and bruised about the head and there are no hopes whatever of her recovering. It is known that Mrs Duffil had a considerable sum of money upon her when she left Hull, but none whatever was found upon her person when she was picked up, so that, no doubt, the perpetrator of the shocking act secured a good booty. And now comes the most extraordinary part of this affair. The villain who threw Mrs Duffil out of the carriage escaped. As the train was slackening speed on arrival at Beverley, a man was seen to jump out of the carriage in which the crime was committed and run away. A cow-keeper, William Holliday, was later taken into custody. Up to 8 o'clock last evening, Mrs Duffil was in a state of insensibility, and suffering from concussion of the brain. Very faint hopes were entertained of her recovery.

At a subsequent inquest held by the local coroner Edward Conyers, the body of Caroline Duffil was formally identified by her husband before the inquest was adjourned. The full inquest resumed at the Beverley Arms Hotel on Friday 4 February 1853, in the presence of a jury. Mr Conyers the coroner presided.

Thomas Duffil, landlord of the Freemason's Arms, Beverley and husband of the deceased gave evidence of identification and the fact that she travelled by train to Hull on the day in question. She was in good health. He told the court that she was not usually in the habit of drinking during the daytime but he was unable to say how much money she had in her possession when she left home. A suggestion was made to Thomas Duffil that his wife was expecting to receive a substantial sum of money owed to her by someone in Hull during her visit but her husband stated that he had no knowledge of this fact and did not believe that she was carrying such money when returning home and he had no reason to believe that his wife had been robbed whilst on the train.

Doctor Samuel Watson gave the following evidence:

I am a surgeon at Cottingham. On the night of Tuesday, the 18 January 1853, I was called to see a woman at the station. I was directed to a point on the line near the warehouse where I found a female in a state of insensibility laid on the ground. On examination, I found her face very much contused, slightly cut with the gravel and blood flowing from the wounds in her nose. I was informed she had jumped from a railway carriage. I had her conveyed to the railway hotel. No one identified her at the time. On searching, I found a leather pocket round her waist, fastened by a strap. It had divisions in it. There were a few cigars and some peppermint drops in one portion. In another division there was 12s (twelve shillings) and some copper (small denomination coins). There was also an envelope in one of the divisions, addressed to Mr Thomas Duffil. I despatched a messenger to that address. It was to the Freemasons' Arms. I remained until about ten o'clock. I left orders that she was not to be removed, as I was fully satisfied that she was suffering from concussion to the brain. She smelt of spirits but I cannot say whether she had drunk to excess.

William Phillips, Station Master at Cottingham gave the following evidence:

I am the Station-Master at Cottingham. I recollect the train coming in on the 18th. When the train started I was near the last carriage. I did not hear any voices coming from the carriage. Shortly after, the porter told me that a woman had jumped out of the carriage and he was going for a doctor. I walked along the track to the deceased and a young man was holding her head. Doctor Watson came and she was removed to Cottingham. A purse and watch were taken from her person (the purse containing £3.16s. 6d was produced).

Asked by a jury member if the compartment door was closed when the train departed, Station Master Phillips replied; I feel quite confident the door was shut when the train left Cottingham Station.

Stephen Matthews, train guard on the train in question gave the following evidence:

> I am a guard on the York and Midland Railway Company and was with the last train on the night of the 18th. There was the engine, the tender, guard's van and five carriages. We arrived at Cottingham at two minutes past seven. I got out of my van and called out the name of the station along the whole length of the train. I was handed a parcel which was going to Beverley. I got onto the foot-board of my van just as it was leaving the end of the platform. I estimate that it would be forty to fifty yards from my van to the end of the train. It is my practice to stand on the foot-board until the carriages are clear. I saw nothing of the accident and knew nothing about it until the next morning. From the distance of my carriage from that in which the deceased was, if she had called out, I would not have heard her. No passengers in any carriage can communicate with the guard.

The Coroner, addressing Mr Locking, a railway official who was present, stated that this incident showed how necessary it was that something should be done in order that passengers on a train are able to communicate with the guard. Mr Locking replied he had no doubt something would shortly be done (referring to the introduction of communication cords or similar devices on trains).

Doctor Sandwith, who carried out a post mortem on the deceased, gave evidence to the effect that Caroline Duffil died as a result of bleeding inside the skull and injuries to the brain caused by her fall from the train. She had also suffered abrasions to her face and body as a result of coming into contact with gravel on the railway track after her fall.

William Brigham, a passenger travelling in a compartment near to the one where the incident took place gave the following evidence;

> I heard a woman scream as the train was leaving Cottingham but I did not see anyone jump or fall from the moving train as it left Cottingham. I did not hear anyone shout the words 'thief' or 'murder'. I did see a man jump out of the train as it slowed down whilst approaching Beverley. I later showed a police officer the precise location where this had happened.

Charles Swift a Police Officer gave evidenced of arresting the suspect Holliday:

> The prisoner asked me what I wanted with him and I told him I wanted to ask him some questions regarding Mrs Duffil. I asked him if he was at Hull that Tuesday and he said he was. He said that he knew Caroline as the Landlords wife and met her by chance in Hull. They had a drink together in the afternoon. I asked him if he came back on the same train with Mrs Duffill that night and he said 'Yes'. They had a glass of brandy and water together at the railway refreshment room in Hull before the train left. I asked him if he came back in the same carriage with her. He said he might have but he could not say for sure as he was very drunk. He did not recollect anything about the train journey except someone calling out the station name 'Cottingham' as it arrived there. He said he was partly asleep. I told him that he was being apprehended for throwing Mrs Duffil out of the carriage. He said 'O dear I don't think I could ever do anything of the kind but I was so drunk I can't recollect anything about it'. That was all the conversation which passed and Holliday was conveyed to York Gaol.

The Coroner in summing up told the jury that he did not believe Holliday ever intended to rob the deceased. It was his opinion that Holliday, if he had done anything at all, had attempted to commit an indecent assault upon her. If he had done so and had caused her to jump out of the train, he would be guilty of manslaughter.

After deliberating, the jury returned a verdict of manslaughter against William Holliday who was committed on a Coroner's Warrant to stand trial. He was remanded in custody.

William Holliday appeared before Judge Baron Martin at the York Spring Assizes on 8 March 1853, charged with the manslaughter of Caroline Duffil. On the direction of the judge, the Grand Jury threw out the bill on the grounds of insufficient evidence. No evidence was offered against Holliday, and he was acquitted of the charge against him.

Like numerous other crimes committed in the Victoria era, it was often extremely difficult for police officers to obtain sufficient evidence to secure a conviction or indeed to bring a case to court. There was no DNA, blood grouping or forensic science which we all take for granted today.

Evidence was in the main provided by eye witness accounts and confessions. Nobody will ever know the full circumstances that led to the tragic death of Caroline Duffil, or any motives which William Holliday may have had. Without a testament from Caroline Duffil, there was never going to be sufficient evidence to convict Holliday of any offences committed against her. Perhaps the intuition of the Coroner was correct in thinking that perhaps whilst under the influence of alcohol, Holliday decided to make advances towards Caroline and subjected her to an indecent assault which resulted in her jumping out of the train compartment.

If, however, Caroline Duffil was thrown or pushed from the moving train, it would make William Holliday a candidate for being the perpetrator of the first ever murder of a passenger on our railways. Nobody will ever know.

Robbery on the London Underground

On the evening of Saturday, 21 August 1880, Clarence Lewis, aged 18, who was employed by Messrs Barnham's, tea merchants of Ravens Road, Spitalfields, East London, visited the premises of another branch of the firm located in Kensington, West London, to collect the cash takings for that week. After collecting £105 (£13,300 today) which was contained in a paper bag, he walked to Kensington railway station in order to catch a train back to Spitalfields with the money. Upon his arrival at the station, he was approached by Stephen Henry Perry, aged 24, of Duke Street, Marylebone. Perry, a well-dressed man, stated that he was a former employee of Messrs Barnham, and was familiar with the fact that a member of staff collected the weekly takings from the Kensington branch of the company on Saturday evenings and conveyed it back to the head office in Ravens Road. Perry, claiming old acquaintance, suggested that rather than travel alone with the cash, he should join him and travel in a first-class compartment, for which he offered to pay. Lewis accepted the invitation and shortly before eleven o'clock, they boarded a train on the Metropolitan Railway to travel towards the city. There were no other occupants in the compartment.

During the journey, Perry produced a bottle of port wine from his pocket, and offered Lewis a drink, which he accepted. Perry then offered him another beverage which Lewis tasted but did not like. Shortly after departing King's Cross Station, whilst in the underground tunnel, Perry attempted to chloroform Lewis who pushed him away. Perry then attacked Lewis and started to beat him violently about the head with a stout walking cane, at the same time kicking him about the body. Lewis was bleeding profusely and the railway carriage was covered in blood. After removing the bag of money from Lewis's pocket, Perry dragged him towards the carriage door, trying to open it whilst the train was in motion in an attempt to throw him out of the compartment. Lewis however continued to struggle with his assailant until finally, he lapsed into unconsciousness and slumped to the floor.

When the train arrived at Aldersgate Street Station (known today as Barbican Station), Perry alighted. Lewis who had briefly regained consciousness managed to stagger from the train behind him and started shouting to attract the attention of station staff and other passengers. Perry started to flee the station but was apprehended by members of the station staff who detained him and summoned the police.

Lewis, who had again relapsed into unconsciousness was conveyed to St. Bartholomew's hospital in a serious condition. Clarence Lewis remained in hospital for three weeks before being discharged, still in a debilitated condition.

After his arrest by police, Perry was searched and his pockets were found to contain a bottle of port wine, a bottle of laudanum, a bottle of chloroform and the paper bag containing the £105 stolen from Lewis.

Stephen Henry Perry appeared before the Guildhall Magistrates Court in the City of London on Monday, 23 August 1880, charged with attempted murder, assault and wounding with intent to cause grievous bodily harm and robbery. He was remanded in custody.

On Wednesday, 15 September 1880, Perry appeared before the Central Criminal Court in London to face the charges. The judge was Mr Justice Stephen. Mr Poland QC and Mr Montague QC acted on behalf of the public prosecutor, with Mr Grain QC representing the defendant. Perry pleaded not guilty on all counts.

The evidence presented was strong and conclusively proved that the defendant Perry was the person who attacked Lewis on the train and stole the money. Upon conclusion of the trial, the jury immediately returned a verdict of not guilty of attempted murder but guilty of assault and wounding, with intent to commit grievous bodily harm and guilty of robbery.

After the verdict was announced, Mr Grain QC addressed the court on behalf of Perry and endeavoured to show that the robbery was not premeditated but was as a result of sudden temptation. Mr Poland QC called a young man named Emmett, an employee of Messrs Barnham, who had also occasionally carried the money from one establishment to the other and he stated that on the previous Saturday when he was so engaged, the prisoner got into the same carriage with him and pressed him to a drink something from a bottle, but he refused.

The judge said he had no doubt that Perry had deliberately planned the robbery and that he had used the most brutal violence in order to carry it out. He said it was the most cowardly and brutal outrage that had ever been brought under his notice and it was hardly possible to believe that a young man like the prisoner, who appeared to have possessed some respectability of position and a certain amount of education, could have been guilty of such a brutal and cowardly act. He had no doubt that after the prisoner had carried out his act of plunder, he had attempted to throw Lewis out of the carriage, utterly regardless of the consequences. Under all the circumstances, he ordered him to receive thirty lashes of the cat (cat o'nine tails) and twenty years penal servitude. The prisoner uttered a scream when sentence was pronounced.

After sentencing Perry to thirty lashes, Mr Justice Stephen told him that it was done:

> … in order that, coward as you are, you may feel the pain and know what it means. The brutality of crime would be lessened if flogging was invariably resorted to. Wife-beaters, maltreaters of policemen and sturdy vagabonds would be speedily reduced in numbers if they knew that detection would be followed not merely by a peaceful seclusion in gaol, but by excruciating pain on their own persons. Those who are most callous of the feelings of others, are frequently most alive to pain.
>
> None but crimes of brutality should be punished in such a way. A codification of lashes according to the enormity of the offence would speedily bring about a respect for the limbs and lives of Her Majesty's subjects.

Perry was removed from the dock to serve his twenty years penal servitude. His flogging was carried out at Newgate prison on Friday, 1 October 1880.

In 1880, like most other railway companies, the Metropolitan Railway had its own railway police force who worked closely with other Metropolitan Railway staff members, including station porters and ticket collectors like those who went to the assistance of Clarence Lewis and detained his assailant until the arrival of the Railway Police. A photograph which appears on the image plates in the centre of the book is believed to have been taken in 1876, just four years before this incident, shows a Railway Policeman posing for a photograph with staff members employed by the Metropolitan District Railway.

Lady Molested by an Army Officer

Judging a person by his or her demeanour or outward appearance can be very misleading. Such was the case when a very gentlemanly and distinguished British army officer boarded a train at Liphook Station in Hampshire. This particular officer however had a much darker side to his character which was only revealed during the fateful train journey that followed. His name was Valentine Baker, a British Army colonel and staff officer stationed at Aldershot Barracks.

Valentine Baker was born in Enfield on the 1 April 1827. His father, Samuel Baker was a prosperous merchant, plantation owner and the founder of an English settlement in Ceylon (now Sri Lanka). He also became a Director of the Great Western Railway Company. His older brother, also named Samuel, would later become Sir Samuel Baker, a well-known African explorer who discovered one of the sources of the river Nile.

At the age of six, Valentine Baker moved from Enfield and spent his early life living in Gloucester, where he attended Gloucester Grammar School. He also spent time in Ceylon and decided at a young age that he wanted to join the military. After completing his education, he joined the Ceylon Rifles, a mounted cavalry regiment, where he served briefly before transferring to the British 12th Royal Lancers cavalry regiment. He saw active service during the Crimean War and was present at the fall of Sevastopol. In 1859, he was promoted to the rank of major in the prestigious 10th Hussars and the following year he was promoted to the rank of colonel in charge of the regiment, a position which he held for the next twelve years.

He then spent some time attached to the German army as an observer, before returning to England in 1874 to take up the position of staff officer at Aldershot. Much of his spare time was taken up in pursuit of horse riding with his high society friends, including the Prince of Wales. In 1875, the fortunes of Colonel Valentine Baker's glittering career were about to take a nosedive as a result of an incident which revealed a much seedier side of his character.

It was in the afternoon of Thursday, 17 June 1875, when Miss Kate Rebecca Dickenson, aged 22, travelled from her home in Sussex to London by train. Miss Dickenson boarded a train at Midhurst and sat in a first-class compartment. The compartment was empty when she joined the train. After a while, the train stopped at Liphook station, where Colonel Baker entered the compartment and sat opposite her. She had never seen him before. Colonel Baker started a conversation with Miss Dickenson, talking first about the theatre, then about his military career. There was nothing untoward about his conduct.

After the train left Woking, the next scheduled stop was Vauxhall, some thirty minutes away. At this point, the conversation between Colonel Baker and Miss Valentine became rather more personal. He stated that he would like to meet her again and asked for her name and address which she declined to give. He persisted in asking for her details which she again refused.

Colonel Baker then stood up and closed the compartment window before sitting down. This time he sat alongside her. There was no arm rest between them. Colonel Baker then took hold of Miss Dickenson's hand but she pushed him away saying he was too close to her. The Colonel then put his arm around her waist and pulled her towards him, kissing her on the cheek. She tried to push him away, but he said; 'You must kiss me, darling.'

Miss Dickenson again pushed him away, got up from her seat and tried to activate a communication device in the centre of the compartment, but it did not respond. Baker said, 'Don't ring, don't alarm the guard.' Baker then forced Miss Dickenson back into the corner of the compartment, pushed her tight against the upright cushions of the seat and stood in front of her whilst kissing her several times on the lips. All the time, his body was pushing up against her in a suggestive manner. Miss Dickenson could not move and with his weight pushing against her she was quite powerless. Baker continued kissing her on the lips before stooping down and placing his hand up her skirt onto her leg, then beneath her under-garments. Miss Dickenson again pushed him away whilst at the same time, attempting to break the glass window with her elbow. This was to no avail. She did, however, manage to open the window. She put her head out of the window and started screaming. Baker pulled her head back into the carriage, but she continued to scream whilst fearing for her life.

Miss Dickenson continued to struggle with her assailant and did manage to turn the door handle inside the compartment and opened the door. She stepped onto the running board of the train and grabbed hold of the outside door handle with one hand and grabbed Baker's arm with the other to prevent herself falling from the moving train. Baker shouted; 'Get in dear, get in.' Another passenger in the next compartment was alerted to the situation and activated the communication device which caused the train to come to a halt close to Esher Station. Colonel Baker said to Miss Dickenson; 'Don't say anything. You don't know what trouble you'll get me into. Say you were frightened. I'll give you my name and anything.'

After the train had stopped, Miss Dickenson was assisted from the train and gave her particulars to the guard of the train. Colonel Baker alighted from the compartment and he was put into a different compartment by the guard. Miss Dickenson re-joined the train and was accompanied for the remainder of her journey by the Reverend J. Brown after stating her desire not to travel in the compartment alone. Upon arrival at Waterloo Station, the train was met by two railway police officers who placed Colonel Baker under arrest.

Details were taken of all witnesses, the principal of whom was the guard of the train, Henry Bayley, who was able to say that Baker's clothing, including his trousers, were disarranged. Other witnesses were a Mr Pike, Mr Burnett and the Reverend J. Baldwin Brown.

During the Victoria era, it was often very difficult or impossible, to secure a successful prosecution against an eminent man, for a sexual assault on a woman. Had the assault taken place in a second, or third-class compartment, against a woman of lower or working-class status, the case would have been much more difficult to prove and is unlikely that the woman would have been believed.

However, the victim in this case was a respectable lady from a distinguished family travelling in a first-class compartment. She had three brothers, one of whom was a physician, another was an army officer and the third was well-respected barrister. She discussed the incident at length with her brothers and sought their advice. As a result of this, she travelled to Guildford the following day, accompanied by her brother and two railway policemen. There, she obtained a warrant against Colonel Valentine Baker.

On Monday, 2 August 1875, Colonel Baker, aged 48, appeared before the Surrey County Assizes in Croydon. Mr Justice Brett presided. The case commenced at 10.30am. Seated near the judge was the High Sheriff of Surrey, Leveson Gower, the Marquis of Tavistock, Arthur Annesley, Viscount Valentia MP, Sir Richard Airey and other distinguished gentlemen.

Mr Poland QC appeared for the prosecution. Mr Hawkins QC, who was considered by many to be the finest defence lawyer in London at the time, represented Colonel Baker. His services had been engaged and paid for by the Prince of Wales himself. He was assisted by Mr Lillie QC. It was reported by the press at the time that the largest crowds ever witnessed at the Assize Court gathered inside and outside the court from eight in the morning to witness the trial. The indictments were laid before the court.

There were three counts; attempt to ravish, indecent assault and common assault. Colonel Baker pleaded not guilty on all the counts.

The trial commenced and Miss Dickenson gave her evidence. She was ushered into court by her mother and accompanied by her three brothers. She was placed in the witness box. One of her brothers was allowed to stand beside her the whole time that she gave her evidence. Miss Dickenson was immaculately dressed in black and gave her evidence in a calm, firm and modest way. She detailed the circumstances in which she made the train journey and repeated the evidence which she had already given in substance when the case had appeared before the Magistrate's Court.

After Miss Dickenson completed her evidence, Henry Bayley the train guard was called, followed by the other prosecution witnesses. Several witnesses gave evidence that when Colonel Baker was put into another compartment, they noticed that his clothing, including his trousers, was disarranged.

The case presented for the defence was, in essence, that what actually occurred within the railway compartment was a complete misunderstanding between Miss Dickenson and Colonel Baker. It was claimed that Miss Dickenson had acted under the influence of exaggerated fear and alarm.

After the judge concluded his summing up, he instructed the jury who then left the courtroom to deliberate. After just fifteen minutes the jury returned to deliver their verdict. Colonel Baker was found not guilty of attempting to ravish, but guilty of indecent assault. The charge of common assault was left on file.

Several witnesses were called by the defence to give a good character reference for the defendant. These included Sir Richard Airey and Lieutenant General Sir Robert Steele, Commander of the British Forces at Aldershot.

On passing sentence, the judge complimented the jury on their verdict. He further remarked that it had been hinted during the trial that the young lady (Miss Dickenson) was wrong to enter freely into a conversation with the defendant in a train compartment and that she might expect to suffer outrage in consequence. The judge said that he considered that to be a libel upon the society to which she belonged. His Lordship continued (addressing Baker);

> It may be suggested that the libertine outrage which you have committed has defiled her. I say distinctly it has not. She walks out of this court pure and innocent and undefiled. The courage she has displayed has added a ray of glory to her youth and innocence and beauty. With regard to you, It seems to me that of all people in that train on that day, you should have been the last person to do nothing but absolutely defend a defenceless woman and I say it advisedly, that even if a girl so young had behaved herself with indiscretion, it was only due, that a person of your age and position should have protected her against herself, but there is nothing in her conduct which can excuse the most dishonourable deed you intended to do. Now it seems to me that if I were to pass a sentence carrying with it all the personal degradation and physical degradation which follows an ordinary sentence, I should be subjecting you to a punishment which in your case would be far greater than it would be to other persons who might be guilty of the same offence. I therefore propose to spare you those physical degradations. The sentence of the court is that you be imprisoned in a way not to be personally degrading to you for twelve months in the gaol of this county. That you be fined five-hundred pounds [£60,000 today]. That you be further imprisoned until you pay that fine. That you pay the costs of this prosecution and that you be imprisoned for a further term not exceeding three months until you have paid those costs.

Applause followed the sentence and the defendant was taken from the dock after a trial which had lasted for seven hours. Colonel Valentine Baker was incarcerated in Horsemonger Lane Gaol, (Surrey County Gaol) at Southwark to serve his sentence. He was dismissed from the British army and his dismissal was endorsed by Queen Victoria herself. Colonel Baker's disgrace was complete.

Upon his release from prison, Valentine Baker emigrated to Turkey where he joined the Ottoman army that was in a military conflict with Russia. After briefly holding a position in the gendarmerie, he was given command of an infantry division and promoted to the rank of Lieutenant General. He was given the name Baker Pasha. Upon cessation of the Russo-Turkish war in 1878 he served in Armenia, before accepting an offer to command a newly formed Egyptian army in 1882. This proposal came to the notice of British authorities who informed the Turkish authorities that they would not recognise Baker as commanding officer of the Egyptian army and that no British officer posted to Egypt would ever serve under him. Consequently, when Baker Pasha arrived in Cairo, the offer for him to command the Egyptian army was rescinded and he was placed in charge of the Egyptian Police Force in an advisory capacity, a position which he held until he died from a fever at Tell-El-Kebir on the 17 November 1887.

Chapter 4

Railway Fraud

The Great Northern Railway Fraud

Perhaps the biggest fraud carried out by an individual against any railway company during the nineteenth century involved the Great Northern Railway Company. The perpetrator of the fraud was Leopold Redpath, who was employed as the principal registrar of stock for the company during the 1850s.

Leopold Redpath was born in Greenwich in 1816. In 1854, he was appointed the registrar of shares and transfer of stock, for the Great Northern Railway Company. His annual salary was £250, the equivalent of £250,000 today.

Redpath was considered to be an honest, upright citizen, involved in many fashionable institutions of the day. He was a fellow of the Royal Institution, the Society of Arts and the Botanical Society. In addition, he was a governor of Marlborough College, St Anne's Society, the Sons of the Clergy, Christ's hospital and six different Orphan Societies.

Shortly after starting work for the Great Northern Railway Company, he embarked upon a large-scale fraud against his company in order to fund a lavish lifestyle. As the principal registrar of stock, he had the entire control of that department of the Company's business. He started out on his fraudulent activities by creating a fictitious shareholder's account under the name of John Morris, from Manningtree in Essex. He opened the account with the amount of £200 of his own money. Later he added a zero to this amount, thus altering the amount from £200 to £2,000. When the shareholders' dividends were paid out, he gained £1,800 (over £200,000 today) on the stock transferred.

He subsequently repeated this with an account in the name of Shaw in the sum of £500, which after again adding the zero became £5,000. He continued repeating this process using different names and fictitious accounts in the sums of £1,000, £1,250 and £1,500. Once again, he added a zero to each of these amounts. His criminal activity meant that for every £100 of stock purchased by him he would receive an additional £900 of stock from the company which he had not paid for.

Between 1854 and 1856, Leopold Redpath had built up a luxurious life style, funded by his criminal activities. He lived in a magnificent fashionable house at 27, Chester Terrace, Regents Park, London, with his wife, Jessie. They employed a cook and twelve servants. The house was fitted out with the finest furniture and the walls were adorned with fine art including some old masters. He had his own private box at the London Opera House and was a frequent visitor to London's theatres. There was scarcely a fashionable party, high society gathering or operatic performance which he did not attend. He paid rent on the house in which he was living, but he owned a similar house in Chester Terrace which was bought and paid for.

He had an alluring country retreat at Weybridge in Surrey, in addition to which he owned a freehold farm at Beadonwell, near Erith in Kent (now Greater London) and six enclosures of building land in Upton Road, Bexley. He owned two villas and a dwelling house, together with several meadows near Elstree and two semi-detached villas and an acre of land in Tottenham. All his land and property was bought and paid for from the proceeds of his fraudulent activities committed against his employer, the Great Northern Railway Company.

In the summer of 1856, the suspicions of the Company Directors were eventually aroused when they realised that the company was paying out dividends for far more than, according to their audited accounts, they were liable for and as a result, they called in the Great Northern Railway Police to investigate. Detectives commenced their enquiries into the matter and Redpath offered to resign. The Company Directors refused to accept his resignation. Enquiries into the background of Redpath quickly revealed that he was living a lavish lifestyle way beyond that of a person of his means. As a result, Superintendent Loxton of the Metropolitan Police at Albany Street Police Station was asked to assist. The Great Northern Railway Police continued to gather evidence of fraud committed by Redpath against the Railway Company, whilst Superintendent Loxton and his officers investigated the background of Redpath. They ascertained the extent of land and property which he owned and they visited his properties with search warrants to glean evidence and record details of the contents in order to establish the extent of his wealth. In November 1856, after a long and painstaking investigation, William Charles Kent, a clerk, and assistant to Redpath, was arrested, together with another clerk, Thomas Hogden, on suspicion of being involved in fraud with Leopold Redpath.

As detectives moved in to arrest Redpath, he managed to evade capture by absconding. Detectives made every effort to trace his whereabouts and they established that he had fled to France on 11 November and was staying with a Mr Strauss in Paris. Superintendent Loxton obtained a warrant for his arrest. Police later received information that Redpath was returning to London to attend to some business, before going back to Paris. Police seized the opportunity and on Friday, 14 November, Redpath was arrested whilst having breakfast at a friend's house in 4, Usher Place, Regent's Park, where he was staying. He appeared before Clerkenwell Magistrates the following morning where he was remanded in custody for three weeks. On 5 December 1856, Redpath and Kent appeared before Clerkenwell Magistrates Court in London charged with fraud. They were committed to stand trial at the Central Criminal Court. Bail was refused. Thomas Hogden did not face charges as it was decided to use him as a prosecution witness.

On 16 January 1857, the trial of Redpath and Kent took place at the Central Criminal Court before Mr Baron Martin and Mr Justice Willes. Both defendants pleaded not guilty on all counts. The prosecution was conducted by Mr Budkin and Mr Gifford. Mr Atkinson represented Redpath and Mr Hawkins and Mr Thomas represented Kent. Upon completion of the case, the jury deliberated before finding the defendant William Charles Kent not guilty on all counts. He was acquitted and discharged. Leopold Redpath however was found guilty on all charges. Mr Justice Willes, after some strong remarks on the enormity of the offences, sentenced Redpath to transportation for life.

Redpath was remanded to Newgate prison but later transferred to Millbank and Pentonville prisons before being transported in 1858 on the vessel *Edwin Fox* from Portland (Weymouth) to the British Penal Colony at Fremantle, Perth, Western Australia. In 1868, some ten years after his transportation, Redpath was granted a conditional pardon and in 1871 he set sail for Sydney in New South Wales. Redpath, who never returned to Britain, remained in Sydney leading an obscure lifestyle until his death at the age of 75 in 1891. He was buried at the Rookwood cemetery in Sydney, Australia.

The total amount of money embezzled from the Great Northern Railway Company by Redpath was never accurately established, but it was a staggering amount, estimated as being in the region of between £200-300,000 (between £22-34 million today).

The London and North Western Railway Fraud

At the same time that Leopold Redpath was defrauding vast sums of money from the Great Northern Railway Company, another fraud was being perpetrated by a senior official employed by the London and North Western Railway Company. His name was Thomas Goalen.

Goalen was born at Leith, Scotland in 1807 and excelled during his school years before becoming a teacher of mathematics. In 1833, at the age of 26, he secured the position of Chief Accountant for a new railway company, the Grand Junction Railway, which operated over a distance of 82 miles (132 km) from Birmingham, via Wolverhampton, Stafford and Crewe, to Warrington. In 1846, the Grand Junction Railway amalgamated with two other railway companies to form a new railway company which was called the London and North Western Railway Company (LNWR). The new LNWR Company rapidly expanded and was the largest railway company in Britain between 1846 and 1922, extending from London through the Midlands and North of England into Scotland as well as incorporating large parts of Wales.

When the company was founded in 1846, Thomas Goalen was offered the position of Chief Accountant and Official Auditor for the whole company, which he accepted. He was based at the London and North Western Railway Headquarter at Euston in London. By the age of 39, Goalen had become the man in charge of the whole finances of the largest railway company in Britain. Revenue staff under his control included auditors, accountants, cashiers and station booking clerks (all staff were male at that time).

Like today, nineteenth-century railway companies received their revenue from two major sources, the main source being the transportation of freight, which included items such as coal and other minerals, parcels, food commodities and the royal mail. The second source of revenue was money received for the conveyance of passengers.

When internal fraud was committed against railway companies by members of staff during the nineteenth century, it usually involved money paid by passengers as fare revenue. Railway staff members such as booking clerks and ticket collectors spent their whole working lives handling cash which they received from passengers and whilst the railway companies relied on their honesty to account for and declare all such money, it was a simple matter for corrupt employees to retain some of the money for themselves, and not pay it in or account for it.

In an attempt to prevent such fraudulent activities happening, strict controls and procedures were put in place which were closely monitored by internal revenue staff. The majority of passenger tickets were issued at booking offices (now commonly referred to as a ticket offices). Each booking clerk was required to account for all the tickets issued by him during his shift, as well as being responsible for his own cash drawer in which he placed the cash takings. All revenue received from passengers were placed in the cash drawer and at the end his shift, the amount of cash had to equate to the numbers and cost of all the tickets issued. All tickets were consecutively numbered.

As well as station booking offices, most large railway stations during the nineteenth century had a cashier's office which handled company finances. Railway cashiers were responsible for handling large amounts of cash as the name suggests. All revenue received at booking offices for ticket sales would periodically be removed from the booking office safes and transferred to a cashier's office. Even at small rural stations, booking offices would send their revenue takings by train to a designated cashier's office at regular intervals. Cash collected by ticket collectors for excess fare payments and issuing tickets to passengers was also paid in to a cashier's office.

The person overall in charge of each cashier's office was designated the Chief Cashier. He was ultimately responsible for paying all cash revenue from passengers into the main company bank account at regular intervals by making the payments through a local bank.

The full circumstances and nature of the fraudulent activities carried out by Thomas Goalen, against the London and North Western Railway Company were never fully established and are subject of some speculation. His downfall however was triggered by events involving a police investigation and subsequent arrest of another employee of the LNWR, a Chief Cashier, William Caitcheon.

Caitcheon was employed as the Chief Cashier at Liverpool Lime Street Station, a busy mainline grand terminus station located in the city centre. He was the person responsible for ensuring that all passenger fare revenue collected at Liverpool and surrounding areas was paid into the LNWR Company account by paying in the money either at the Bank of Liverpool or the Moss Company Bank, both located in Liverpool city centre. He then submitted the necessary accounting documents to Thomas Goalen at the railway headquarters in London to confirm that the transactions had been carried out.

During the early 1850s, however, it appears that Thomas Goalen discovered some discrepancies in the accounts which he was receiving from William Caitcheon, the Chief Cashier at Liverpool. Consequently, Goalen visited the cashier's office in Liverpool un-announced and carried out an audit check. It is assumed that the audit confirmed that Caitcheon, had been embezzling money from the company, although the audit carried out by Goalen was never published or disclosed to the company directors in accordance with normal procedure. Instead, it appears that Goalen confronted Caitcheon directly with his findings and the two men came to a private agreement which allowed Caitcheon to continue his fraudulent activities, provided Goalen himself was given share of the proceeds. Goalen subsequently turned a blind eye to any discrepancies in the accounts being submitted by Caitcheon.

Unfortunately for the two men, not long after Goalen had visited Liverpool, a routine audit was carried out by the railway audit department at Liverpool Lime Street Station Booking office. The booking office was just one of a handful chosen at random from the hundreds of booking offices on the LNWR network. During the audit, one transaction revealed that ticket sale revenue received by booking clerk Thomas Caton on two consecutive days, did not appear to have been paid in to the company accounts. Caton was interviewed by audit staff, after which they were satisfied that his accounts were in order and that the cash which he received had been paid into the cashier's office. Further follow up checks were carried out at the cashier's office where discrepancies were uncovered which suggested that not all the revenue arriving at the cashier's office was being paid into the company's bank account. The matter was reported to the London and North Western Railway Police based at Liverpool Lime Street who were close to hand, and they started their own investigation into the allegations.

In January 1854, Caitcheon, the Chief Cashier responsible for paying all passenger revenue into the company's bank account was interviewed by police. He stated that all monies received from passenger revenue had been paid in to the company accounts, with the exception of a small percentage which was routinely withheld, to fund an approved company bonus scheme authorised by Thomas Goalen, the Chief Accountant. He went on to say that he himself, in his capacity of Chief Cashier, was allowed to retain a percentage of company profits as a bonus payment and regular sums of money were also paid into a private bank account belonging to Goalen who was also entitled to receive bonus payments. Despite protesting his innocence, Caitcheon was arrested and later charged with the embezzlement of cash from his employer.

Thomas Goalen was also arrested on suspicion of stealing cash from his employer. When the evidence was placed before him, he immediately admitted his guilt. He further admitted being fully aware that the revenue accounts submitted by Caitcheon and endorsed by him as being correct, had been falsified.

Unlike the Great Northern Railway Fraud perpetrated by Leopold Redpath, it was decided that the police investigation into the fraudulent activities of Goalen and Caitcheon would go back just twelve months prior to it being reported to police. During that period of time however, it was estimated that the money stolen by the two men may well have been the region of £10,000 (over £1 million today).

On 30 March, 1854, Thomas Goalen and William Caitcheon appeared before Mr Justice Cresswell at the Liverpool Spring Assizes. The prosecutor was Mr Dearsley QC. Goalen was represented by Mr Senior QC and Caitcheon was represented by Mr James QC.

Goalen was charged with larceny servant and embezzlement involving the sum of £6,000 (£698,000 today). He pleaded guilty and was sentenced to fourteen years transportation.

Caitcheon was charged with two counts larceny servant and embezzlement involving the sums of £596 (£69,393 today) and £51 (£6,000 today). He pleaded not guilty to both charges but was found guilty by a jury and sentenced to four years penal servitude.

The court was told that, at the time of the offences, both men were employed by the LNWR Company. Goalen was employed in a top job as Chief Accountant and Official Auditor of the company whilst Caitcheon was a Chief Cashier. Both men were subsequently dismissed from the service of the London and North Western Railway Company.

Forging the Transfer of Railway Stocks and Shares

The railway boom years of the 1840s saw the emergence of railway fraudsters and it was quickly realised that fraudulent activities would be a huge cause for concern as the railways expanded. There is no doubt that a large number of offences involving various aspects of fraud went undetected, particularly in the early years of railway development. The procedures surrounding the issuing of stocks and shares was just one example where money could be swindled from railway companies and frauds of this nature continued to take place throughout the nineteenth century. Three typical examples of fraud involving railway stocks and shares are briefly outlined below.

On 7 May 1889, Thomas Barton aged 46, a silk manufacturer from Macclesfield in Cheshire, appeared before the Central Criminal Court in London, having been charged with forging the transfer of London and North Western Railway and North Staffordshire Railway stocks to the value of £35,000 (over £4.7 million today), during a sixteen-year period between 1870 and 1886. Barton pleaded guilty and was sentenced to ten years penal servitude.

During the same decade, John Duncan, Chairman of the Greenock Railway Company in Scotland, appeared before Lord Young at the Glasgow Circuit Court on Monday, 23 December 1878 charged with issuing false share certificates from the Railway Company of which he was the Chairman. The court heard that Duncan netted himself £11,444 (over £1.4million today) by issuing false shares over a nine-year period whilst he was the secretary of the company.

When people in authority use their position of trust to promote criminal activities for personal gain, it is frowned upon by the judiciary who take an extremely dim view of the matter which is often reflected in sentencing. This case was a typical example and there was no Christmas cheer for John Duncan when he was sentenced to life imprisonment with hard labour after Lord Young told him 'this is the worst case of forgery I have ever dealt with'.

Gordon Whitworth appeared before the Central Criminal Court on 15 September 1885 charged with forging a London and North Western Railway share certificate valued at £300 (£40,500 today). He was sentenced to five years penal servitude.

The Railway King

The 1840s was the decade of 'Railway Mania' in Britain, when railway construction was at its peak and railway share prices rocketed towards a record high. The situation of Britain's railways by the end of 1844 was 2,235 miles (3596.884 km) of track in operation and an additional 855 miles (1375.99 km) in various stages of construction, having been approved by parliament, making a grand total of 3,090 miles (4982.873 km). A total of 104 different railway companies had been founded and were operational. Some investors were being offered as much as ten per cent interest return on their capital if they invested in railway shares, as money poured in from speculators.

In 1845, no less than 383 applications were presented to parliament for the building of new railways. The following year saw the pinnacle of Railway Mania when a staggering 560 new railway schemes were laid before parliament, 270 of which were authorised and received Royal Assent, authorising the construction of an additional 4,540 miles (7,306 km) of new track.

As the year 1846 came to a close, however, people started to sell their railway shares when it became apparent that the large dividends which they had been promised were not forthcoming. There were also rumours involving fraud and over-investment, some of which were exposed in the highly respected *The Times* newspaper.

Between 1847 and 1850, the gravy train came to a halt and the Railway Mania bubble burst. Share prices dropped dramatically and many people lost their life savings, although a lucky few did make their fortunes. Others were declared bankrupt. Almost 100 new railway construction schemes which had already been approved by parliament or given Royal Assent were abandoned due to lack of finance. The golden years for railway investors seemed to be at an end.

Without a doubt, the most infamous of all the early railway speculators and fraudsters of the railway boom years, who did make his fortune, was George Hudson, dubbed the Railway King. George Hudson was born at Howsham near York in 1800. At the age of fifteen, he moved into the City of York to start work as an apprentice linen draper with the firm Bell and Nicholson, in College Street, York. He completed his apprenticeship in 1821, after which he married Elizabeth, the daughter of Richard Nicholson, one of the business partners. Later, the other business partner, William Bell retired and George Hudson was given his share of the business and the firm became Nicholson and Hudson.

In 1827, George Hudson, who was by then already a wealthy man, received a bequest of £30,000 (almost £3.4 million today) from a great-uncle, Matthew Bottrill, a gentleman farmer. In 1833, he decided to invest the money in a venture which proposed the building of a railway from Newcastle to London via York. An enabling Act of Parliament was passed in 1837, and the York and North Midland Railway Company was subsequently founded. George

Hudson was the largest shareholder in the company and he became the Company Chairman.

George Stephenson, the famous locomotive engineer, was appointed Chief Engineer of the company. In November that year, Hudson was appointed Lord Mayor of York before going on to become a Tory Member of Parliament for Sunderland. Hudson soon became a millionaire and continued investing his fortunes in railway companies which earned him the unofficial title of the Railway King. He also purchased land and several private estates within his home county of Yorkshire.

George Hudson was well established as the Railway King by 1844, when he owned over 1,000 miles of railway track. He continued to buy shares in railway companies and it was alleged that he distributed several thousand pounds in bribes to politicians and others in order promote the railway companies in which he had financial interests. Although the mid-1840s saw the zenith of railway mania, it was about to yield unwelcome changes to the good fortunes of George Hudson.

George Stephenson had become suspicious of Hudson's business methods and no longer wished to be a part of them, so he resigned his position with the York and North Midland Railway Company. By the late 1840s, cracks began to appear in George Hudson's empire after he was found to have been paying dividends out of company capital, which was unlawful (Railway Clauses Consolidation Act 1845, Section 121). As his empire crumbled around him, he fled to France to avoid his creditors. He later returned to Britain where he was arrested and imprisoned for three months in his home city of York. Criminal proceedings against Hudson for his fraudulent activities would have caused a great deal of embarrassment, both for the government and his many influential friends, so he was able to stave off prosecution by offering financial settlements to investors who had lost money as a result of his actions. In one respect, George Hudson was a very lucky man. His power, influence and friends in high places had undoubtedly prevented him from serving a very lengthy prison sentence. After his release from prison, Hudson lived a sedate life in a modest property in London. With his vast fortune gone, he died in 1871, leaving an estate worth a moderate £200 (£25,000 today) a far cry from the rich pickings of the former millionaire.

Although the fraudulent activities of George Hudson are believed to have been considerable, they were never fully investigated at the time, in part due to his status but also due to the means available for dealing with complex fraud cases. Both railway police forces and civil police forces were still in their infancy and consisted primarily of uniformed officers who seldom carried out in-depth investigations into crimes. Criminal Investigation Departments (CID) were not introduced until the early 1860s and whilst some small detective departments were just beginning to emerge in various railway and civil police forces in the 1840s, large scale complex frauds were seldom reported to police and as such were never fully investigated. A number of perpetrators of early frauds used this to their advantage and as such, became wealthy individuals.

Embezzlement

Stealing money from an employer by way of fraud. A simple, yet typical example of this type of crime occurred in the small, picturesque village of Hele in North Devon in 1850, when a railway staff member fell foul of the law due to the vigilance of a railway police superintendent. The circumstances surrounding this case are as follows.

Robert Walters was employed as a porter/ticket collector at Hele Railway Station in North Devon. He had worked on the railway for seven years. Hele Station was located on the main Bristol to Exeter railway line between Taunton and Exeter. Walters however, was not the honest and polite railway servant that he purported to be and he exploited his position in order to embezzle cash from his employer.

His downfall resulted from the vigilance of Superintendent Blackmore of the Bristol and Exeter Railway Police, who happened to alight from a Bristol train at Hele railway station one chilly autumn morning in 1850. As he went to leave the station, a passenger in front of him presented a ticket to Walters. The ticket was issued at Bristol that morning for a journey to Taunton. Walters charged the passenger the excess fare between Taunton and Hele, then put the money and the Bristol to Taunton ticket in his pocket. Superintendent Blackmore's suspicions were aroused by his actions and he ordered some ticket tests to be carried out on him.

Over the next few weeks, undercover officers of the Bristol and Exeter Railway Police purported to be members of the travelling public. They alighted from trains at Hele station when Walters was on duty and either presented him with a ticket which required excess payment, or they stated that they had travelled from stations without having purchased a ticket and offered to pay the outstanding fare. In all cases, Walters accepted fare payment or excess fare payment without issuing a ticket or giving a receipt. The results of the ticket tests were later analysed and the suspicions of Superintendent Blackmore were proved to be well founded. Walters had failed to pay any of the money to his employer, or account for it. He had pocketed the cash for himself. Walters was arrested for embezzlement of cash and committed for trial by local magistrates. In December 1850, Robert Walters, having pleaded guilty to offences of embezzlement was sentenced to ten years transportation after the judge told him he would not tolerate a man in a position of trust stealing from his employer.

As well as ticket collectors, station booking clerks involved in the issue of tickets to passengers spent their entire working lives handling cash. Whilst most booking clerks on the railway were honest hard working individuals, a few bad apples emerged from time to time, who could not resist the temptation to pocket some of the cash which passed through their hands.

The Distribution of Counterfeit Coins

Whilst the most common form of dishonesty involving booking clerks related to the embezzlement of cash, various other crimes have been carried out over the years by booking clerks endeavouring to make some extra money. One interesting and rather unusual case occurred during the nineteenth century when a railway booking clerk came under suspicion for offences relating counterfeit currency.

Arthur Keen, aged 32, was employed as a booking clerk by the Metropolitan Railway Company at Edgware Road railway station in London. In the spring of 1875, a barman in his local public house introduced Keen to John Neave and his fiancé Annie Bolwell. The barman informed Keen that John Neave, who was a shoemaker by trade, may be able to put some money his way. Keen listened to what Neave had to say and showed an interest in his idea about making some money.

It transpired that Neave, a shady individual, was engaged in the production of counterfeit coins of the realm. The coins were of different denominations. An agreement was reached between the two men that Neave would supply counterfeit coins to Keen, who would exchange the coins for an equivalent amount of genuine money from the booking office. Keen would then hand out the counterfeit coins, together with genuine coins as change to unsuspecting passengers who had purchased tickets. Thousands of people were purchasing tickets from Edgware Road booking office every day, most of whom were in a hurry and just put change into their pockets without making a close examination of it. There were also occasions when Keen worked at other booking offices, in particular Westbourne Park, which would enable the source of the distribution of the counterfeit currency to vary.

The devious scheme was put into action and a considerable number of counterfeit coins began to circulate in London. As time went on, Keen distributed more and more counterfeit coins into public circulation without arousing any suspicion. Eventually, some members of the public started complaining that they had received bad money from the Metropolitan Railway Company. Detectives from within the company started an investigation in which they began visiting booking offices, buying tickets and checking the coins handed back in change. One detective received a bad shilling in change after tendering half a crown to buy a ticket at Edgware Road station. Consequently, Edgware Road booking office was soon identified as a possible source from where the coins were emanating. Detectives carried out observations and quickly established a link between Keen and Neave. They saw both Neave and his fiancé Bolwell visit the booking office either together or on their own, on a number of occasions and hand Keen a number of small packages, for which he gave them money. By 11 May 1875, detectives had enough evidence to incriminate Keen, Neave and Bolwell, who were subsequently arrested.

The three prisoners were charged with conspiring to utter (tender) counterfeit currency. It was estimated that Keen had been circulating approximately 500 counterfeit coins each week from the booking office. The three defendants pleaded guilty in court and John Neave was sentenced to seven years penal servitude. Annie Bolwell was given twelve months penal servitude and Arthur Keen received two years penal servitude. After the convictions, the circulation of counterfeit coins in the area abruptly stopped.

Fare Evasion

Ticket offences and fare evasion have always been numerically the most common examples of fraud committed against any railway company, resulting in a direct loss of revenue. Whilst a considerable number of passengers defraud railway companies in this manner on a daily basis, the true extent of revenue loss, and the numbers of offences actually committed by this type of activity can never be established, as many of the ticket frauds committed pass by undetected.

During the nineteenth century, these offences were often investigated and dealt with by detectives. However, as the years passed by, the numbers of ticket offences being committed became so numerous that specific departments were set up to deal with them. Some were manned by railway police, others by railway revenue staff. This eased the burden on detectives who were then able to concentrate on the more serious types of frauds as well as other serious crimes which were being committed.

Unfortunately, no amount of publicity will eradicate fare evasion on the railways. Members of staff and railway passengers alike, old or young, male or female it makes no difference, a whole range of individuals engage in the practice. People even try to evade paying fares for their dogs. For whatever reason, fare evasion has occurred since the dawn of the railways and as long as the trains keep running, the fare dodging brigade will be lurking amongst the passengers.

During the nineteenth century, early railway legislation was introduced for dealing with fare evasion, but it was the introduction of the Regulation of Railways Act of 1889, which created a wider range of specific offences for the different methods used by passengers in order to avoid payment. This act of parliament has stood the test of time and is still in common use today.

Of the specific offences contained within the 1889 act, by far the most common offence committed can be found under Section 5 (3a) of the act, which makes it an offence for any person to travel or attempt to travel upon the railway without having previously paid his or her fare and with intent to avoid payment. Paying the fare means paying the full fare for the journey. Offenders are usually punished by way of a fine and ordered to pay compensation for the loss of the fare revenue. A term of imprisonment, however, is an option if deemed necessary.

Station Master Catches a Fare Dodger

On Friday, 20 December 1861, Jonathan Leonard boarded a train on the South Wales Railway at Newport in Monmouthshire without having purchased a ticket. He travelled to Magor railway station, where he alighted from the train. Instead of going through the ticket gate, Leonard went behind some trucks and climbed over the fence. Thomas Wellington, the Station Master at Magor witnessed the incident and followed Leonard to the Lion Inn public house located in the village of Magor. There he confronted Leonard who admitted travelling from Newport, stating he had lost his ticket. The station master reported Leonard and when the case came before the Newport Magistrates, Leonard pleaded guilty to travelling without a ticket with intent to avoid payment. He was fined the sum of twenty shillings and ordered to pay costs.

Adult Travelled on a Childs Ticket

At 10am on Tuesday, 1 June 1858, Henry Challenger, a respectably-dressed man, arrived at Bristol station on an excursion train from Birmingham. As he passed through the ticket barrier, he handed a child's ticket to Richard Wright the ticket collector. Wright stopped Challenger and pointed out that he had tendered a child's ticket costing one shilling and six pence, instead of an adult ticket which costs four shillings.

Wright asked Challenger for the difference in the fares but Challenger refused to pay. After refusing to give his name and address, he was detained and taken before Bristol Magistrates. Challenger told magistrates that the reason he bought a child's ticket for one shilling and six pence was that in Birmingham, posters advertised excursion trains running from Birmingham to Bristol on the first and second of June priced at one shilling and six pence. This price also included admission to Bristol Zoological Gardens for the sum of three pence. He offered to leave a sum of money with the magistrates if they released him to allow him to telegraph Birmingham and obtain a copy of the poster advertising the special offer.

The magistrates, after a lengthy discussion, told the defendant that the case against him had been proved and it was their intention to fine him twenty shillings plus costs. The magistrates stated that he would be required to pay the fine but it would be held by the clerk of the court and if he could prove within a reasonable time that the excursion offer he referred to was genuine and that he had no intention to defraud the railway company, his money would be returned to him. The money was then handed over to the clerk of the court by Challenger, who left the court and was never seen or heard from again. The special excursion offer referred to by Challenger did not exist.

Racegoer Only Pays for Part of His Journey

Shortly before 7.30pm on Friday, 21 October 1892, Police Constable Smurthwaite of the North Eastern Railway Police was on duty at Darlington Station when he saw John Griesdale alight from a northbound passenger train along with numerous other passengers who were returning from a race meeting at Thirsk. He recognised Griesdale as a dubious character who was well known to police.

Constable Smurthwaite watched as Griesdale went into the refreshment-room before going to the booking office to purchase a ticket. He then boarded a Bishop Auckland train which was standing in the station. Constable Smurthwaite boarded the train, approached Griesdale and asked to see his ticket. He produced a single ticket from Darlington to Bishop Auckland. Asked if he had another ticket, he replied 'No'. Griesdale was arrested and taken into custody where he admitted having attended the race meeting at Thirsk, before travelling back to Darlington without paying his fare and attempting to avoid payment. He subsequently appeared before Darlington Magistrates where he was fined £2 (£260.00p today) plus costs.

Forged Railway Tickets to Avoid Paying His Fare

On 26 January 1876, Frederick Margetson, aged 22, a draughtsman, appeared before Wolverhampton Magistrates Court, charged with forging a number of London and North Western Railway tickets.

The court heard that Margetson travelled daily by train between Dudley and Birmingham, using railway tickets which he himself had forged by hand. He had a remarkable ability to copy genuine LNWR train tickets using a pen. It was almost impossible to detect that the tickets were forged, without the use of a magnifying glass. The forged tickets were only discovered after they had been used and sent to the London ticket audit office together with all other spent or used tickets. The ticket numbers were then seen to coincide with the numbers of genuine tickets from which they had been copied.

Enquiries by London and North Western Railway Police subsequently led to the arrest of Margetson who was subsequently committed by the Wolverhampton Magistrates to stand trial at the next assizes. Margetson, of previous good character, later appeared before the Staffordshire Lent

Assizes where he pleaded guilty to forging a number of railway tickets. He was sentenced to six weeks imprisonment.

Jockey Comes A Cropper

At 5.45am, on Wednesday, 23 September 1868, James Quinlen a 25-year-old professional jockey, went to Bishopsgate (now called Liverpool Street) Great Eastern Railway Station in London to catch a train to Newmarket to take part in a race meeting. He was in company with two other men. The three men went to a platform ticket gate and Quinlen asked the ticket collector if he could board the Newmarket train with the luggage, whilst the other two men went to the booking office to purchase the three tickets. The ticket collector agreed, and Quinlen boarded the train with two large pieces of luggage.

A short while later, the other two men returned from the booking office and showed their tickets as they passed through the barrier. They did not show a third ticket in respect of Quinlen. Just before the train was due to depart, the ticket collector went to the compartment where the three men were sitting and asked to examine their tickets. The two men who had earlier produced tickets at the ticket barrier produced them again and the ticket collector saw one of the men then pass his ticket to Quinlen, which he then produced. The ticket collector asked to see all three tickets at the same time but only two could be produced. Quinlen then said he thought his friends had bought him a ticket.

Quinlen was informed that he would be reported for attempting to travel upon the railway without having paid his fare and with intent to avoid payment. He subsequently appeared before the local magistrate's court where he pleaded guilty to the charge. He was ordered to pay a fine of twenty shillings (£120 today), or serve seven days imprisonment. The fine was paid.

Chapter 5

Pickpocketing

Another form of stealing which was often encountered on the railway during the nineteenth century was stealing items from the person, or pickpocketing as is was commonly called. Pickpocketing was an extremely common crime in the nineteenth century, occurring on an almost daily basis. Pickpockets were usually found wherever crowds of people gathered, such as fairgrounds, markets, race meetings, theatres and of course, railway stations. Many of the railway pickpockets were career criminals often well known to police as they travelled up and down the country, stealing from unsuspecting members of the public at every opportunity.

The art of pickpocketing was often practised by boys from a young age in the nineteenth century as famously portrayed in the 1838 novel *Oliver Twist* by Charles Dickens. These impoverished boys often continued their criminal activities throughout their lives and were generally well known to police. Railway pickpockets were no exception. They favoured the railways due to the crowds of people who travelled daily. Young men frequently travelled on crowded trains which were taking passengers to and from race meetings and other sporting events where rich pickings could be found. Football supporters became easy targets towards the end of the nineteenth century as they returned home from matches after celebrating success or drowning their sorrows in defeat. Some pickpockets preferred to work alone whilst others worked in teams or gangs. The judiciary viewed pickpockets with contempt and severe sentences were often handed out to persistent offenders.

Purse Stolen at London Bridge

A typical example of early pickpocketing and subsequent sentencing which occurred on the railway took place in September 1849 when Mrs Elizabeth Young travelled by train from Croydon to London Bridge on the London, Brighton and South Coast Railway. Shortly after leaving London Bridge Station, she felt a tug on her clothing. She turned around and saw two men. One of the men introduced himself as a railway detective and the man with him was Michael Daley who was under arrest. The officer told Mrs Young that Daley had stolen her purse whilst she was leaving the railway station. Mrs Young checked and found that her purse containing 8/10d had indeed been stolen. The purse and contents were found in the possession of Daley. It transpired that Daley was part of a gang of pickpockets operating on London Bridge Station that day and as a result of a number of recent complaints from members of the public, railway detectives had been observing the station in an attempt to apprehend offenders. Daley had been seen approaching several female passengers before removing the purse of Mrs Young. Michael Daley, who had several previous convictions for pickpocketing, appeared before the Surrey Quarter Sessions on Thursday 25 October 1849 and was sentenced to seven years transportation.

Transportation as a punishment in Britain was abolished by the Penal Servitude Act of 1857, although some convicts continued to be transported until 1868 when the last transportations took place from Britain. After that, incarceration with hard labour or penal servitude as it was called was a favoured sentence handed out to criminals convicted of what were considered to be serious crimes, including that of pickpocketing.

Female Pickpockets

As mentioned earlier, pickpockets often started their trade at a tender age and whilst the majority of these pickpockets were young boys, girls were sometimes found to be the culprits. Ordinary railway passengers may view some young men with suspicion but would seldom give a young girl a second glance if she was tagging along behind or alongside another female passenger. One young girl used this trait, together with the hustle and bustle of Glasgow Buchanan Street Station to her advantage.

Janet Macfarlane, an inconspicuous 13-year-old, was sent to Glasgow Reformatory for five years in July 1899, after stealing purses containing substantial sums of money, by picking the pockets of well-dressed ladies as they passed through the station. A police spokesman told the court that despite her tender years, she was one of the most expert pickpockets they had ever encountered.

Although pickpockets were predominantly men, some women did continue the trade through their adult lives. One such serial pickpocket well known to police was Mary Ann Langford from London who was sentenced to twelve months hard labour, after she was apprehended at King's Cross station whilst attempting to steal from passengers travelling on the Great Northern Railway.

Railway Pickpocket Feigns Madness

In August 1856, a notorious railway pickpocket by the name of Jakes was sentenced to four years penal servitude at the Devon County Quarter Sessions. After convincing the authorities that he was completely mad, he was removed from the county gaol and admitted to Exminster Lunatic Asylum, near Exeter. A few nights later however, it appears that he had a 'lucid interval' and his mind was completely restored. Ensuring that the coast was clear, he decamped from the asylum and was not seen or heard of again.

Pickpocket Steals a Gold Watch

At about 8.30pm, on Sunday, 12 August 1877, Donald Fraser, a commercial traveller, was standing on the platform of the London and South Western Railway station at Kew Bridge in the company of some ladies, awaiting the arrival of a train to London. A train arrived and as Mr Fraser was looking for a first class compartment, he heard a 'click' and immediately noticed that his watch-chain was hanging down from his waistcoat and his solid gold pocket watch missing from the end of it. At the same time, he noticed a man drawing his hand away. He quickly grabbed hold of the man and accused him of stealing his watch. The train guard came to his assistance and the man was detained, pending the arrival of the police. The watch was found on the station platform nearby.

A 22-year-old cabinet maker, John Milton, was charged with stealing the gold watch, valued at £25 (£3,000 today). He later appeared before the Middlesex Quarter Sessions where he pleaded guilty to the charge. Detective Constable Richard Kenwood told the court that he had known Fraser for fifteen years and although he had no previous convictions, he was an associate of thieves and his wife was currently under sentence of penal servitude for felony. Due to him having no previous convictions, he was sentenced to six months penal servitude.

Purse Stolen from Passenger on a Train

On 8 September 1874, George Williams, age 23, appeared before Justice Harrison at the Surrey Quarter Sessions, indicted with stealing a purse containing ten shillings (£60 today) from the person of Emma Overall. Mr Lilley prosecuted and Mr Maceby defended. The prisoner pleaded not guilty to the charge.

In her evidence, Miss Overall, a young woman, stated that on the evening of the 13 August 1874, she got into the third class carriage of a train at Surbiton to travel to London. Also in the carriage was the defendant Williams. When the train reached Vauxhall station, Williams got up from his seat and sat beside her. When the train arrived at Waterloo, Williams pushed past her and she felt a tug at her dress pocket. She immediately realised that her purse, which contained ten shillings, had been stolen. She jumped out of the train and as Williams ran away, she shouted, 'Stop that man, I've lost my purse.' Williams ran through the booking hall with Miss Overall in pursuit. Police Constable Bentham of the London and South-Western Railway Police who was on duty at the station, heard Miss Overall shouting and upon seeing Williams running through the booking hall, stood on the exit stairs to block his escape. With the assistance of another officer, Williams was arrested. A search was made, but the purse and contents were never found (possibly picked up by another passenger). Upon completion of the case and after a short deliberation, the jury found Williams guilty as charged.

Police Constable Lockyer, the court officer, stated that he had known the prisoner since he was a child. He had commenced stealing at an early age and had been frequently convicted. He was a well-known railway thief and in 1863, he was sentenced to six months imprisonment for a similar offence of stealing a purse from a lady in a railway carriage.

Chief Superintendent James Purchase, of the Reading Police, stated that Williams was a well-known thief who operated under the aliases of Bennett, Miller, Brown, Smith, Austin and Clark. In the main, he committed robberies in railway carriages and was often accompanied in these operations by a woman. In 1866, he was tried and convicted at Reading Assizes and sentenced to seven years penal servitude. Williams also had numerous previous convictions dating back to his childhood.

The prisoner then looked in a threatening manner towards the witness and shouted; 'I would not be here now if it wasn't for you. You won't let me earn an honest living.' Mr Justice Harrison reminded the prisoner that he had been found guilty on clear evidence and stated that he should not flinch from his duty, as he sentenced him to ten years penal servitude and seven years police supervision.

James Argent – Master Pickpocket

One of the most audacious railway pickpockets of the nineteenth century was James Argent, who is thought to have stolen many hundreds, if not thousands of wallets, purses and watches over a period of almost forty years, between 1860 and 1900. Argent was a well-dressed, well-spoken individual of gentlemanly appearance. With his utmost coolness, he brought pocket-picking and watch-snatching to something approaching a fine art.

Argent did serve a number of terms of imprisonment, but each time he was arrested he used a different alias, including the names Groves, Saunders, Wilson, Barton and Day. He first came under notice of the authorities in 1868 when he received twelve months hard labour at the North London Quarter Sessions. In 1873 he appeared before the Surrey Quarter Sessions after some 200 cases of daring thefts from the person were traced to his skilful hands. Even though he was sentenced to eight years penal servitude, it did not deter Argent from his criminal activities. Upon his release from prison, he resumed his old career and actually boasted that within three hours of leaving prison, he had secured two gold watches.

One infamous trick which he performed during his life of crime occurred at Paddington Railway Station in London, after he entered a first class compartment of a West of England express passenger train. Argent sat quietly in the corner reading a newspaper until he heard the guard's whistle signalling the departure of the train. Suddenly, he stood up and said, 'Good gracious, I'm on the wrong train.' Argent then brushed hurriedly past the other passengers, opened the door and jumped out of the compartment whilst the train was moving. A short time later, as the train was speeding towards Reading, two of the gentlemen passengers he had brushed so hastily against, found that they had both been relieved of their gold watches.

James Argent continued his life of crime well into his sixties, but as the turn of the nineteenth/twentieth century approached, he disappeared into obscurity and was never seen or heard of again.

Chapter 6

Obstructing the Railway

Apart from two trains colliding head on, perhaps the most dangerous accident which can occur on the railway is when a train, travelling at speed, encounters an obstruction on the track. Many obstructions on the railway are unavoidable. They can be caused by falling trees, landslides, floods, snow and other natural phenomena. Apart from the obvious physical danger to passengers and train crews when locomotives encounter objects on the track, widespread delays and disruption can be caused, often affecting whole railway networks. Dealing with the simplest cases of railway obstruction invariably causes train delays and considerable expense to the railway operating companies involved.

Obstructing the railway can also be a very serious criminal offence. Deliberately placing objects on the railway line for whatever reason can lead to serious train derailments and in some cases widespread loss of life. The penalty for obstructing the railway with intent to endanger life is that of life imprisonment. Of course, there are varying degrees of railway obstructions which have been subject of railway legislation for many years. Not all obstructions are carried out intending to cause loss of life or serious injuries to people. The criminal offence of obstructing the railway falls into various categories, some of which do not have to be intentional. A railway can be obstructed by neglect or negligence on behalf of an individual. For example, should a workman who is engaged in the maintenance or repair of a railway line, forget to remove his tools after he has finished work and inadvertently leaves them on the track, thereby causing delay or accident involving a train, he would be guilty of a criminal offence of obstructing the railway by neglect.

Obstructing the railway by wilful omission is another example of criminal obstruction of the railway. If a person uses an unmanned railway crossing, of which there were many in the nineteenth century, and does not bother to close the gates, thus allowing animals to stray onto the railway line, thereby causing a train to slow down or stop, that person would be guilty of an offence of obstructing the railway by an act of wilful omission i.e., omitting to fasten the gates after use.

The obstruction itself does not have to be a physical obstruction. Interfering with signals or stealing line-side copper cable or telegraph wires, are criminal offences in their own right, but the subsequent delays that these acts cause to trains also constitute an additional criminal offence of obstructing the railway by an unlawful act. Even the offence of trespassing upon the railway, which is, in itself, an unlawful act, can lead to a person being prosecuted for obstructing the railway if a train had to slow down or stop as a consequence of the trespassers being on the track. All nineteenth-century railway companies were obliged to exhibit trespass warning notices upon the railway, especially at railway stations. This still applies today.

Offences of obstructing the railway, have unfortunately been an all too common occurrence since railways were first introduced in the early nineteenth century. Fortunately, death and serious injuries resulting from these acts have been relatively few.

In the early years of railway construction, railway policemen and watchmen were placed at intervals of a mile or so along a railway line, specifically to ensure that the trains did not encounter obstructions. The rapid expansion of the railway network, combined with improvements in signalling and track safety soon rendered this practice unnecessary and it ceased after a few years, although to this day it has remained an integral part of a railway policeman's duty to ensure passenger safety which includes dealing with obstructions on the railway lines.

Even the introduction of railway policemen and watchmen at regular intervals along the track when the railways were first established did not guarantee that the railway would not be obstructed, as directors of early railway companies soon found out to their dismay.

The first deliberate obstruction of a railway is thought to have occurred on the Liverpool and Manchester Railway in the afternoon of Wednesday, 22 December 1830, just three months after the railway opened. The *Meteor* locomotive left Liverpool for Manchester, with a train consisting of just four passenger carriages. The train was preceded by the *Rocket* locomotive, acting as a pilot engine which was a light engine with no coaches or wagons attached, travelling ahead but in sight of a train, to ensure that the track was safe and free from any obstructions.

As the trains approached the bottom of an incline at a location known as Mr Bourne's Colliery, at Sutton, four labourers working near the railway picked up a small stage wagon (intended to be used for the carriage of goods) and waited until the pilot engine had passed before placing it across the rails. They also placed a large iron switcher bar across the track. A watchman, who was stationed to protect that part of the line, remonstrated with the men but they ignored him. He even attempted to remove the obstructions but the men threatened him and prevented him from doing so. As the train rapidly approached the obstructions, the watchman began waving his arms frantically at the locomotive in order to make the driver aware of the danger and stop the train. This signal however was either misunderstood or given too late because the train did not slow down and came in contact with the wagon and the iron bar. The collision caused the *Meteor* locomotive to become detached from the carriages and career down an embankment into a field some six or seven feet below.

The carriages themselves were dragged off the rails but did not career down the embankment and fortunately, there was no loss of life. The driver of the *Meteor* suffered severe chest injuries after being thrown violently forward into the controls of the locomotive, but the fireman alighted from the locomotive relatively unscathed. Several passengers sustained minor injuries, whilst others suffered the effects of shock and concussion.

In the meantime, the crew of the *Rocket*, having lost sight of the train behind them, reversed backwards to ascertain what had happened to it. Upon reaching the scene, the driver and fireman of the *Rocket*, together with the fireman from the *Meteor* and with the assistance of a number of passengers, managed to get the de-railed carriages back onto the railway lines. The driver and fireman of the *Rocket* coupled their engine to the carriages and the train continued its journey to Manchester, where it arrived a little over one hour late. There seems little doubt that the four workmen who carried out this appalling act did so with the intention of causing serious injury or loss of life but their motives for doing so remain a complete mystery. The culprits evaded justice by escaping across some fields, never to be seen again.

In the incident just referred to, the objects which were used to obstruct the railway belonged to the railway company itself. As the years passed, it became fairly common for railway obstructions to consist of railway materials lying close to the track, because they were convenient to use and close to hand.

Materials were often delivered to lineside locations in advance of maintenance work being carried out and old materials removed or being replaced were often left alongside the track until it was convenient to collect and dispose of them. As a result, many items deliberately placed on the railway lines had been left there by track maintenance workers and other railway staff members.

Sacked Railway Employee Wanted Revenge

In April 1868, Samuel Jenkins, aged 33, a former railway guard was seen placing stones and pieces of iron across the railway line on the Great Western Railway line at Kidderminster, shortly before an express passenger excursion train was due. When approached, he ran away but was later apprehended. During an interview with police, he stated that he was seeking revenge against his former employer, the Great Western Railway Company, who had dismissed him from his job as a railway guard a few months earlier.

Jenkins appeared before the Worcester Assizes on 17 July 1868, where he pleaded guilty to obstructing the railway with intent to endanger passengers. The learned judge told him that if he had not been interrupted whilst he was in the act of placing obstructions on the line, there was little doubt that a deplorable catastrophe would have occurred. He went on to say that the offence was a most grievous one and one in which he was bound to press the full penalty of the law. He sentenced Jenkins to penal servitude for life.

A number of former disgruntled railway employees during the nineteenth century were convicted of this and other types of offences against railway companies as acts of reprisals after being dismissed for misconduct or other transgressions.

Obstructing the London and South Western Railway

Dawn was just breaking on a cold damp November morning in 1894, as a goods train rumbled along the London and South Western Railway through Fleet in Hampshire. Suddenly the engine driver heard a bang and he brought the locomotive to a halt. The driver climbed down from his cab, walked back along the track and found that some wooden fence palings had been placed across the railway lines. The palings had been crushed and mangled by the train but the locomotive and wagons were unscathed. After removing the remains of the palings from the track, the train continued its journey.

A short time later, the morning milk train was making its run. As it approached the same spot, the driver encountered a similar obstruction. On this occasion, the driver observed a railway sleeper placed across the rails. He immediately applied his brakes but the locomotive struck the sleeper with a shudder and a loud bang. The train somehow managed to remain on the track but extensive damage was caused to the locomotive. Both incidents were reported to the London and South Western Railway Police at Winchester.

Shortly before five o'clock that afternoon, just as darkness was falling, the London to Bournemouth passenger express was speeding through Fleet at about fifty miles per hour when to the screams of passengers, another loud bang was heard and the train came shuddering to a halt. The engine driver climbed onto the track and found the remains of what appeared to be a newly creosoted sleeper jammed between the bogie wheels of the engine and the wheel guard on the front of the locomotive. The wheel guard was extensively damaged by the impact. Later an Exeter express train suffered an almost identical fate, after striking a new wooden sleeper. Once again, the impact was felt by passengers on the train, a number of whom were quite badly shaken.

Extensive enquiries were made by police and an 18-year-old labourer, Charles Wyatt was subsequently arrested. Wyatt was placed in a police cell, alongside another prisoner, Mr Etheridge who had been arrested earlier in connection with another matter.

Etheridge later became a witness against Wyatt and gave police a statement regarding a conversation which took place between them in the cell, after Wyatt told Etheridge he had been arrested for putting things on the railway track. Etheridge told Wyatt that he did not think it was right to obstruct the railway as it was an offence next to murder. Wyatt is alleged to have replied, 'It would be a good job if a few people were killed.' Wyatt was also alleged to have told Etheridge that after he placed the obstructions on the track, he sat on the fence to see what would happen when the train crashed into them.

Charles Wyatt appeared before Mr Justice Cave at the Winchester Assizes on Tuesday, 5 February 1895 where he pleaded guilty to maliciously placing obstructions across the railway at Fleet. Mr Bullen, who appeared on behalf of the prosecution, outlined the facts and told the court that it was a mercy there was not a wholesale slaughter of passengers that day. The prisoner it was said, was of previous good character.

In passing sentence, Mr Justice Cave said it was shocking to think of the slaughter which the prisoner's actions might have caused and if the accused had been a man of full age the sentence would have been a long one. It was of the greatest importance to society in general that persons travelling on business or pleasure should be protected from such scoundrels. The prisoner was still young, but an example must be made of him. Wyatt was then sentenced to five years penal servitude. When the sentence was read out, the prisoner appeared to treat the matter with indifference.

Young Boys Obstruct the Midland Railway

On Wednesday 9 September 1874, two boys, aged 12 were sentenced by Bradford Magistrates to one month imprisonment and four years detention in a reformatory for placing railway sleepers across the line of the Midland Railway near Bradford station three days earlier. The train driver of an approaching train who witnessed the boys committing the act was able to stop his train and remove the sleepers before an accident occurred.

Boys Obstruct the Lancashire & Yorkshire Railway

On Saturday, 10 June 1882, Salford Magistrates ordered that two boys, the sons of a boatman, be whipped for placing large stones and pieces of timber on the Lancashire and Yorkshire railway line near Pendleton, Clitheroe in Lancashire. The sentences were later carried out.

Removed Some Track to Derail a Train

In January 1848, William Scott, age 26, appeared before the Glamorgan Quarter Sessions charged with removing two lengths of railway line from the Taff Vale Railway near Merthyr Tydfil, thereby endangering the safety of railway passengers. He pleaded not guilty.

The court heard that Scott, a native of Aberdeen, moved to Merthyr Tydfil in South Wales in the summer of 1847 and obtained employment as an assistant plate layer employed by Warren and Denroche, a private company who had been contracted by the Taff Vale Railway Company to lay the railway lines of the new Rhondda Valley branch line which was in the early stages of construction from Newbridge (renamed Pontypridd in 1856) to Treherbert.

Scott quickly struck up a friendship with Eliza Williams, a local girl who became his girlfriend. Sometime later however, Scott discovered that a locomotive fireman by the name of Lewis who worked for the Taff Vale Railway Company, was also seeking the affections of his girlfriend, which resulted in the two men having several altercations. On one occasion, Scott even made a threat to kill Evans, in the presence of several witnesses.

On 8 December 1847, Lewis was working as the fireman on a locomotive which was hauling the 6.30pm passenger train from Cardiff to Merthyr. The train consisted of eight coaches which contained some fifty to sixty passengers. It was a dark and stormy evening. As the train was about six miles from its destination in Merthyr, it travelled slowly around a curved length of track cut into the side of a mountain which was located on the left-hand side of the train. On the right-hand side of the train was a steep railway embankment which sloped away from the mountain side, down to the river Taff, which flowed in the bottom of the valley, some 50ft (15.2m) below the railway.

Suddenly there was a loud bang and the train shuddered from side to side. Passengers screamed as the engine, tender and three carriages shook violently, before leaving the rails. Fortunately, the engine, tender and de-railed coaches, having left the track, came to rest on the left-hand side of the line next to the mountain and not on the embankment side where it would have most likely plunged down the embankment into the swollen river below.

The locomotive, tender and three derailed coaches remained upright and the other five coaches stayed on the track. The guard of the train quickly ran from his rear guard's van to the front of the train and to his utter amazement, he found that two lengths of rail, both 15ft (4.6m) long, had been completely removed from the track. One rail was lying half way down the embankment and the other had been left in between the two running rails. It was quite clear to the guard that the two lengths of rail had been deliberately removed, as the bolts were missing from the metal plates which joined the lengths of rail together. The location suggested that the intention by the perpetrator/s was to send the train crashing off the mountainside into the river below but luckily the train derailed next to the mountain and not onto the embankment.

Enquires later revealed that William Scott had been seen in close proximity to the scene of the accident, not long before it had taken place. He was subsequently arrested and although he denied being responsible, he was unable to give a satisfactory account as to why he was seen by witnesses in the vicinity of the incident on a dark and stormy night, almost five miles from his home.

Although pleading not guilty when he appeared in court, Scott was found guilty by a unanimous verdict returned by the jury after a short deliberation. The foreman of the jury then addressed the judge to the effect that some members of the jury were unhappy with the fact that the maximum sentence which could be given to Scott for obstructing the railway under the general railway acts (at that time) was just two years imprisonment with hard labour. They considered such a sentence to be too lenient. The judge however stated that there was no doubt about the murderous intention of the prisoner and that section 166 of the Taff Vale Railway Act gave him the power to sentence Scott to seven years transportation and he felt bound to apply that power. William Scott was duly sentenced to seven years transportation. He showed no emotion and no remorse.

Chapter 7

Crimes Resulting in Accidents

Modern day railways are considered a safe form of transport and fortunately major railway accidents and fatalities are extremely rare. That has not always been the case and a considerable numbers of accidents, including fatalities, occurred on Britain's railways during the nineteenth century. They were due to a variety of causes.

Sadly, some accidents are unavoidable and nobody is to blame. Natural phenomena such as floods and landslides have contributed towards railway accidents over the years. Other railway accidents however which could have been avoided were often caused by the actions of railway staff members albeit not intentionally.

Since the building of the first railways, rules and regulations have been issued to all railway staff regarding the dos and don'ts whilst performing their duties. In 1840, a Board of Trade was set up by the British Government and Her Majesty's Railway Inspectorate was created in order to oversee the safety of Britain's Railways. All railway companies were obligated to report certain accidents to the inspectorate who would then conduct an independent enquiry, before reporting their findings directly to the government.

Since then, a considerable amount of legislation has been introduced regarding the regulation and operation of the railways. Safety has always been paramount on the railways and criminal offences have been created to protect members of the public, passengers and even staff members themselves whilst on the railway. Offences such as manslaughter and endangering the safety of passengers are usually preferred against railway employees when it is believed that their negligence, breach of rules, regulations or other actions have caused accidents which have sometimes resulted in injury or the loss of life. Employees most susceptible to prosecution in such cases, by virtue of their particular jobs, were signalmen, track maintenance workers, locomotive drivers and crossing keepers.

Track Foreman Charged with Manslaughter

On Monday, 26 November 1860, Mr Samuel Hindley, a railway foreman in charge of a gang of platelayers, was sent to a location between Atherton and Leigh in Lancashire (now Greater Manchester) to carry out maintenance repairs on the track. The gang arrived on site shortly after 3pm and made the necessary preparations to replace a section of railway line. The weather was cold and wet, but visibility was fair. A passenger train was due to pass the site where the men were working at 3.40pm, so it was after that train had safely passed by that the repair work was to be carried out.

The passenger train arrived at the location as scheduled and after it had cleared the area, Samuel Hindley and his men went onto the railway line and started to remove sections of the track.

After three sections of track had been completely removed and before the new sections could be put in place, Mr Hindley saw a goods train in the distance approaching from the direction of Atherton. He was taken completely by surprise, as he was not expecting any traffic being in the vicinity during the time it would take to effect the necessary track repairs.

The approaching goods train was in fact running very late. The train, which was travelling from Atherton to Liverpool and consisted of fifty-seven wagons, being hauled by two locomotives. It was well over an hour late, which was extremely uncommon in those days. It should have passed the site at 2.50pm that afternoon, before the permanent way gang had even arrived on site to carry out their repairs.

Mr Hindley instructed a member of his gang to run along the track towards the train and warn the driver. This he did and although the man waved a red flag frantically at the engine driver, he was unable to gain sufficient distance from where the repairs were being carried out to prevent an accident taking place. The heavy train was running down a steep incline and the slippery state of the rails meant that an accident was inevitable. As the permanent way gang members fled for their lives, the train arrived at the spot where the rails were missing and entered the gap. The first locomotive turned completely over and the second locomotive came to rest on its side, partly on top of the first one.

The wagons which formed the train were derailed and piled up one on top another, completely blocking the line. The driver of the first locomotive, John Elliott and his fireman John Valentine, seeing that an accident was unavoidable, had jumped from their engine before the impact. Driver Elliott suffered severe lacerations to his upper thigh and sustained a broken ankle. He had numerous cuts and bruises and was suffering from shock. His fireman John Valentine also suffered severe contusions, but his other injuries were less serious.

The crew of the second locomotive did not have such a lucky escape. Because their view of the track was impeded by first locomotive in front of them, they could not see that an accident was about to occur and had no opportunity to jump from the engine. They both experienced the full force of the impact. Richard Higginson, the driver, aged 42, was believed to have been killed instantly and his body was recovered several hours later, having being found mutilated amongst the mangled debris of the wagons. Remarkably, his fireman was thrown from the cab of the locomotive on impact and emerged from the wreckage relatively unscathed. The guard of the train also escaped unhurt.

An inquest into the death of driver Higginson was held at the White Horse Hotel at Leigh, on 6 December 1860. Evidence was presented before the jury that Samuel Hindley, the foreman of the permanent way gang of platelayers, was in clear breach of railway rules and regulations by not sending two lookouts to place red flags on the track at distances of 500 and 1,000 yards in each direction, from the site where track repairs were being carried out. These flags should have been in position prior to the start of any track repairs to warn the drivers of any approaching trains that it was unsafe to proceed, thus preventing any such accidents taking place.

Further it was said that in addition to the breach of rules and regulations, Hindley, had contravened the Railway Byelaws which were made under the authority of an Act of Parliament, thus making him guilty of an unlawful act. It was suggested to the coroner's jury that if these breaches contributed to the death of driver Higginson, then Hindley would be guilty of manslaughter. The jury returned a unanimous verdict of manslaughter against Hindley and the Coroner committed him to stand trial at the forthcoming Liverpool Assizes. He was granted bail.

On 20 December 1860, Samuel Hindley, aged 52, appeared before Mr Justice Keating at the Liverpool Assize Court, charged with the manslaughter of Richard Higginson. Several of the witnesses giving evidence, including the civil engineer of the London and North Western Railway Company, spoke of the exemplary character of the prisoner.

At the conclusion of the trial and after a short deliberation, the jury returned a verdict of guilty against Samuel Hindley but recommended him to mercy. His Lordship, in passing sentence, spoke of the necessity in dealing with such cases, so as to protect the public but said that in consequence of the prisoner's good character, he would only award him three months imprisonment with hard labour.

The following year, the Offences against the Persons Act of 1861 was introduced in which, sections 32 to 34 of the act, created specific railway offences appertaining to endangering the safety of persons upon the railway. Those sections of the act have stood the test of time and are still in use today.

Justice Should Be Seen to Have Been Done

On Friday, 15 January 1847, at 5.15am, five horses and carts arrived at a railway crossing in Calverley Lane, adjacent to Calverley Bridge Railway station, on the Leeds and Bradford railway line. It was a dark, foggy winter's morning. The level crossing had gates on both sides of the railway lines, to prevent persons using the crossing whilst trains were passing. The Leeds and Bradford railway line had recently been built, having opened just six months earlier on the 1 July 1846.

Finding that the gates were wide open and no warnings or signal lights exhibited, the owners of the horses and carts proceeded to cross the railway lines, but before the rails could be cleared and without warning, a Leeds to Bradford parcels train appeared out of the darkness. The train ploughed through a horse and cart which was being driven by David Anderson. The horse was killed instantly, the cart was demolished and Mr Anderson, who was propelled along the track by the impact, suffered appalling injuries and was rendered unconscious. He was taken to Leeds Infirmary where he later died.

At 9.30am on Friday, 22 January 1847, an inquest was held in the Leeds Court House, presided over by Mr Blackburn, the County Coroner. George Goodman, the Mayor of Leeds and William Rand, Director of the Leeds and Bradford Railway Company were also present. Mr Blanshard of the Northern Circuit appeared as Counsel to observe proceedings on behalf of the railway company. Mr J.N. Barratt, solicitor, appeared on behalf of the relatives of the deceased, and Mr Booth, solicitor, represented Mr Farrar, who was the employer of the deceased and the owner of the horse and cart which was involved in the collision.

The court heard that the deceased, David Anderson was a 45-year-old widower and father of three children, who, by his untimely death, had been left almost destitute. Until the time of his death, Mr Anderson had been employed as a carter in the service of Benjamin Farrar of Rawdon. He was a keen and conscientious worker.

Evidence was presented to the inquest by William Smithson, a farmhand employed by Mr Myers, a farmer from Rawdon, who stated that at 5am on the morning of the accident he left Rawdon in company with fellow farmhand Henry Parker and the deceased David Anderson. They had five horses and carts between them. Smithson and Parker each had two horses and carts in their care and Anderson had one at the rear. They were going to Gildersome to pick up coal. They arrived at the railway crossing at 5.15am, the crossing gates were wide open to allow road traffic to cross the railway line, no warning lights were exhibited and there was no sign of the railway porter, so they assumed it was safe and proceeded to cross the railway.

It was very dark and foggy. Smithson and Parker were just clearing the level crossing when Smithson saw a train rapidly approaching the crossing out of the darkness but the engine did not sound its whistle. Smithson shouted to warn Anderson of the approaching train but the next thing he heard was a loud crash and he realised that Anderson had been knocked down by the train. The horse lay dead on the crossing and Anderson was driven approximately twenty yards along the track by the impact. He was found alongside the line underneath a part of his cart, with the remainder of the cart being completely demolished. Smithson and Parker carried Anderson back to Calverley station platform and then Smithson went for a doctor. David Anderson was later conveyed to Leeds Infirmary but died shortly afterwards. He never regained consciousness. Parker corroborated the evidence of Smithson.

Mr Allison, a house surgeon at Leeds Infirmary gave evidence that Anderson arrived at Leeds Infirmary at about 7am on the 15 January. He was barely alive when he arrived and died shortly after admission. An examination revealed that as a result of the accident, he had suffered compound fractures of the right leg, a dislocation of the collarbone and a severe fracture to the base of the skull, extending to both ears. Doctors at the hospital were satisfied that the cause of death was as a result of severe concussion of the brain arising from the violence which had produced the fractures.

The coroner then stated that there was no doubt as to the cause of death, but it would be necessary to determine whether the railway company and its staff had taken the most effective steps to avoid such an accident.

Matthew Crabtree, the Station Master at Leeds, was called to give evidence of procedures in relation to level crossings. In his evidence, Crabtree stated that the railway porters at Calverley station were on duty from 5.30am until 10pm and it was their duty to keep the gates closed to road traffic when trains were approaching. It was accepted by the railway company, that the crossing was un-manned between 10pm and 5.30am the following morning. On the morning of the accident, a porter by the name of Smithies would have commenced duty at 5.30am but the accident happened prior to his starting work, so he would not have been required to be at the crossing at the time of the accident.

Mr W.T. Adcock, Superintendent of both the Midland Railway and Leeds and Bradford Railway told the inquest that goods and passenger trains approaching the crossing were restricted to speeds of thirty miles per hour and may pass the crossing travelling at that speed. A driver had no specific instructions to sound his whistle upon approaching the level crossing. When the Bradford line was first opened, experienced drivers from the Midland Railway were used to drive the locomotives. Adcock stated that numerous railway crossings are not manned twenty-four hours a day but during the times they are un-manned, the gates would be locked to prevent their use by vehicles and pedestrians crossing the railway. He went on to say that in his opinion, it was the duty of the porter to see that the gates at Calverley crossing were locked in the same manner.

Mr F.M. Young, the resident engineer of the Leeds and Bradford Railway told the inquest that drivers on the Bradford line adhered to the regulations of the Midland Railway Company, where it was the usual practice for the driver to sound the whistle when approaching a level crossing, although there were no specific instructions in respect of that in the rule books of the Leeds and Bradford railway.

Mr Young further stated that the driver of the locomotive involved in this collision was Jessie Gee, a steady and reliable man who had been driving on the line since it opened in July the previous year. He went on to say that an Act of Parliament was in place in relation to the procedures governing all level crossings involving public roads, but he maintained that the act did not apply to this particular level crossing, because committees both of the House of Commons and the House of Lords had declared that this road was not a public highway, but an occupation road.

The Coroner then clarified this point, stating that if this level crossing had been designated a public highway, it would have been compulsory to keep the gates locked, but because Calverley crossing was deemed to be on an occupation road, the Act did not specifically include it. The Coroner told the jury that it was necessary therefore to enquire whether sufficient care had been taken by the Leeds and Bradford Railway Company at the crossing to prevent accidents taking place.

In his summing up, the Coroner told the jury that there was no doubt that the death of David Anderson was caused by the train and that the jury must decide whether the engine had come into contact with him in a purely accidental manner, or whether the company or one or more of their servants were culpable. The road at the crossing was not designated a public highway and therefore they could not allege that porter Smithies had neglected his duty by failing to lock the gates.

The jury would have to decide whether the company had adopted such precautions as were necessary for the safety of the public and he felt bound to state that because the gates were not locked, it was his view that porters should have been stationed to watch this crossing day and night.

It was clear that the engine driver could have prevented this accident by using the locomotive whistle as he approached the crossing. He also quoted from a drivers' rule book entered in evidence by the railway company. Rule number seven stated that 'a driver was required to keep a good look out at all times the engine was in motion. Drivers must exercise caution when approaching a crossing'. The jury must also consider whether the driver passed the station at an unreasonable speed, or if this accident would have taken place if he had used due caution in these matters, if he had not used such caution, then they might return a verdict of manslaughter against him. If, however, they were of the opinion that he was mistaken as to where he was, or had endeavoured to slacken speed, but inadvertently had not done so sufficiently, then they would find a verdict of accidental death.

The jury retired at 2.30pm and returned one hour later to deliver their verdict. They returned a verdict of manslaughter against the engine driver Jessie Gee. They also considered that the Leeds and Bradford Railway

Company were also to blame as they had shown great carelessness in the management of the level crossing at Calverley Bridge. Jessie Gee, the train driver, was then indicted to stand trial for manslaughter.

On Monday, 8 March, 1847, Jessie Gee appeared before the York Spring Assizes, charged with the manslaughter of David Anderson. Charges had not been preferred against any other member of staff, any other representative of the railway company or the company itself. The Jury ignored the indictment and Gee was discharged. Effectively, the case against driver Gee was dismissed, due to lack of evidence.

In today's climate, it seems unthinkable that an accident of this nature could ever have occurred, whereby after a verdict of manslaughter being handed down by a coroner's jury and criticism made of the railway company concerned, neither the company or any member of its staff were held accountable for the tragic death of a 45-year-old hard working widower, which resulted in his three children, who had suffered the loss of their mother, quickly followed by the death of their father through no fault of his own, finding themselves homeless penniless and destitute. Surely, a stain on Victorian society.

Fatal Accident on Railway Viaduct

There were numerous occasions during the nineteenth century when railway employees did stand trial for criminal offences after being considered responsible for causing a particular accident. A considerable number, after having been convicted, felt aggrieved that they had been used as scapegoats or singled out for prosecution when other people, often of a higher status, who they considered equally blameworthy, did not face criminal charges. A typical example of this occurred when Henry Benge, a railway platelayer foreman, was indicted by a coroner's court to stand trial for manslaughter following an accident which took place in 1865 which he felt was not entirely his fault.

On Friday, 9 June 1865, at 3.15pm, a South Eastern Railway passenger boat train travelling from Folkestone to London was derailed whilst crossing the Beult Viaduct near Staplehurst in Kent. The train, which consisted of twelve passenger coaches, was travelling at approximately 20mph. Although the locomotive was derailed, it remained upright on the viaduct together with three coaches. The remaining nine coaches plunged from the viaduct a distance of some 10ft (3m) into the bed of a shallow river below. A total of nine passengers on the train were killed and almost fifty were injured, some seriously.

One of the passengers on the train, travelling in a first-class compartment, was the renowned author, Charles Dickens, who was returning home from a visit to France. He was one of the lucky passengers in one of the three coaches which remained upright on the viaduct and he was unscathed. He climbed out of a carriage window and assisted rescuing other passengers from the train. He later gave assistance to injured passengers before continuing his journey to London on a replacement train. Dickens later wrote his own account of the incident in which he stated that the effects of the accident remained with him forever and he avoided further journeys by train whenever possible as he felt very nervous and uneasy about travelling on the railway.

Enquiries into the accident showed that an earlier track inspection revealed that a length of railway line on the viaduct near Staplehurst was badly worn and in need of replacement. As a result, a gang of platelayers attended the location on the 9 June to carry out the work. The person in charge of the workers was foreman Henry Benge. The maintenance gang, including Benge, were under the control of a permanent way inspector, Joseph Gallimore, who had the overall responsibility for all track maintenance workers and their work, although he personally did not carry out the repairs and was not required to be on site when the actual work was being done.

The time allotted to carry out this particular job was one hour in total, which was ample time to complete the task and clear the railway line. It was the duty of Henry Benge, as the foreman of the gang, to check the times of all trains scheduled to run along the track and select a suitable time between trains when there would be a gap in excess of one hour to complete the work.

Benge decided to carry out the work between 2.30pm and 4pm on Friday 9 June. He worked out that the first train to use the line after 4pm would be the Folkestone to London boat train which departed Folkestone at 4.30pm and was due to cross the viaduct at 5.15pm.

What Benge failed to realise was that whilst checking the train timetable he made a serious error. Instead of checking the column for Friday, 9 June, he checked the next column which showed train times for the following day, *Saturday,* 10 June. The Saturday boat train did cross the viaduct at 5.15pm as the timetable showed but, on a weekday, (including Friday, 9 June), the boat train departed Folkestone two hours earlier at 2.30pm and was due to cross the viaduct at 3.15pm and not 5.15pm as Benge assumed. The scene had been set for a potential disaster.

Shortly after 2.30pm on 9 June 1865, Benge and his workmen arrived at the Beult viaduct to carry out the track repairs as planned. In accordance with regulations, Benge instructed two members of his workforce to walk away from the viaduct in opposite directions along the railway track and place red flags on the track at 500 yards (457m) and 1,000 yards (814m) intervals on both sides of the viaduct to act as a warning to any unexpected or unscheduled approaching trains that work was being carried out on the track and it was unsafe for trains to proceed. Any train drivers approaching the viaduct from either side would have applied brakes to their locomotives upon seeing the 1,000 yard flag and stopped their train accordingly. The second danger flags displayed at 500 yards from the site of the track repairs were an extra precaution for drivers, to prevent any trains from reaching the viaduct where the repairs were being carried out.

Unfortunately, the two men instructed to carry out these tasks only placed a red flag at 500 yards from where the track repairs were being carried out. They did not bother to walk the extra 500 yards to place the second red flags on the track at 1,000 yards.

Henry Benge was unaware of this and assumed the two danger flags were positioned on either side of the viaduct in accordance with his instructions when his gang started their repairs by removing a worn section of the track. At 3.15pm, Benge was astonished to see a passenger train in the distance heading towards the viaduct. What was more alarming was that it was travelling on the Up-line from which the section of worn track had just been removed. The approaching train was in fact the 2.30pm Folkestone to London boat rain, running on time.

With a section of track on the viaduct already removed and the new section not yet in place, Benge immediately ordered a member of his staff to run along the track with a red flag to warn the train driver of the impending danger and stop the train. This was in vain, as the train was already too close and travelling too fast to enable it to stop. The driver later admitted seeing the flag on the track at 500 yards, at which point he shut off the steam and applied the brakes, but he had insufficient distance before reaching the viaduct, in which to stop the train in time. The train speed did reduce from 50mph but was still travelling at about 20mph when the accident took place. Had the 1,000-yard flag been displayed in accordance with regulations and the instructions of foreman Benge, the train would have come to a halt before reaching the viaduct and the accident would never have occurred.

A coroner's inquest was later carried out into the deaths of the nine victims killed in the accident, which resulted in Henry Benge and his boss Joseph Gallimore being indicted to stand trial for manslaughter.

On Wednesday, 26 July 1865, Henry Benge and Joseph Gallimore appeared before Mr Baron Piggott at Maidstone Assizes, charged with the manslaughter of nine persons at Staplehurst on 9 June 1865. They both pleaded not guilty. After addressing the jury, Justice Piggott directed them to acquit the defendant Gallimore as there was no case against him due to insufficient evidence. Gallimore was subsequently found not guilty and the case against him was dismissed.

The case against Benge was proceeded with and following a full hearing, Henry Benge, a hardworking man of impeccable character was found guilty of manslaughter and sentenced to nine months imprisonment. No other charges were preferred against any other railway official or against the South Eastern Railway Company.

Mr Ribton QC, acting on behalf of Henry Benge, had argued that Benge had instructed staff to place flags at 1,000 yards and 500 yards either side of the viaduct to warn drivers of any approaching trains of the repairs being carried out. Had these instructions been adhered to, the accident would not have occurred.

He further stated that Benge alone should not shoulder full responsibility for causing this tragic accident for which he was being made a scapegoat. Members of the jury, however, appear to have taken a different view.

Train Driver Ignored a Danger Signal

On Friday, 24 July 1857, George Tolson, aged 25, a goods train locomotive driver employed by the North Eastern Railway Company was in charge of a general goods train consisting of twenty-eight wagons and vans being transported from Hull goods depot near the Humber estuary along the Victoria branch line to Victoria dock. Tolson had been a qualified engine driver for just two years after serving for a number of years as a locomotive fireman. He was familiar with the track as he regularly worked trains on this particular stretch of railway line.

Tolson left the goods depot at about 4.15pm and proceeded towards Victoria dock. Upon approaching West Parade railway junction, Tolson drove his train past a danger signal which was warning him to stop his train to allow a passenger train to pass through the junction on the main line in front of him. The passenger train was in fact the scheduled 4.30pm local service from Hull to Beverley comprising six passenger carriages, the engine of which was being driven by Benjamin Fowler, a man with eleven years driving experience.

Fowler later gave evidence before York Assizes, in which he stated that as he approached the junction, he sounded his whistle before passing through it at a speed of just six or seven miles per hour. He went on to say that as his train entered the junction, he saw the goods train coming from another direction but assumed it was stationary at the signal as it did not appear to be moving.

The goods train being driven by Tolston was however moving, albeit slowly, and when Tolson noticed the passenger train, he shut off the steam and applied the brakes. Unfortunately, his train was already too close to the junction to stop and a collision was inevitable. His train ploughed straight into the side of the passenger train. William Kemp, a signalman working at the junction left his signal box, approached Tolson and asked him why he had failed to stop his train at the danger signal when he was approaching the junction. He initially replied that the signal was showing 'line clear'. The signalman told him to walk back and look at the signal and he would see that was still in the danger position. Tolson then said, 'The signal must have been partly on and partly off.' An examination of the signal later revealed that it was in perfect working order.

William Rayner, a railway branch line superintendent, later spoke to Tolson about the accident and he gave evidence in court that Tolson had informed him that he had seen the danger signal but thought it would change to line-clear if he drove past it slowly which he had done a couple of times in the past without having to stop his engine.

One of the passengers travelling on the passenger train that day happened to be John Yates, a regular commuter on that particular train. He frequently used the service to travel home from work to the village of Cottingham about

4 miles (6km) outside Hull. Unfortunately, Yates was sitting in a first class passenger carriage which bore the full impact of the locomotive being driven by Tolson. The carriage was crushed by the locomotive and Yates suffered severe injuries to his head and body, as well as compound fractures to some of his limbs. He was rescued from the wreckage in a state of unconsciousness and taken to a nearby house. A local doctor was summoned and treated Yates but sadly he died from his injuries a short time later.

On Wednesday, 5 August 1857, an inquest into the death of John Yates was held at Hull Town-hall before John Joseph Thorney the borough coroner. Following a verdict by the coroner's jury, George Tolson was indicted to stand trial on a charge of the manslaughter of John Yates. He was refused bail and remanded in custody to appear before the York Winter Assizes later that year.

On Monday, 7 December 1857, Tolson appeared before Mr Justice Williams at the York Winter Assizes where he pleaded not guilty to the charge of manslaughter. After hearing all the evidence, the judge was in the process of summing up to the jury when the foreman of the jury interrupted him and said that the jury had already made up their minds that Tolson was guilty of manslaughter, and they did not need any time in which to consider their verdict. The foreman stated that the jury did not wish to trouble his lordship any further, other than to say that they expressed a recommendation for mercy in this case on the grounds that the North Eastern Railway Company had permitted their trains to be managed in a loose and careless way and should shoulder some of the blame themselves.

His lordship stated that whilst he had sympathy for the prisoner, he had to take into consideration the thousands of people who travelled by train and whose lives could be put into danger by the negligence of engine drivers. He felt therefore that it was his duty to impose a severe sentence. He went on to say that because Tolson had already been remanded in prison for five months awaiting his trial and that the jury had recommended him to mercy, the sentence of the court was that he be imprisoned for a further six months with hard labour. He was escorted from the dock.

Signalling Error Costs Lives

Shortly after 6pm on Wednesday, 14 January 1880, a head-on collision occurred between two passenger trains at Burscough in West Lancashire, which resulted in the death of nine people. Over fifty others were also injured, some of them seriously.

The accident happened after a local passenger train service departed Burscough Junction railway station bound for Liverpool some sixteen miles away. The train in question had arrived at Burscough from Liverpool at about 5.45pm on the northbound railway line and remained standing at the station platform, waiting to return to Liverpool at 6.05pm. After departure, the train should, upon leaving the platform, have been diverted by the signalman from the northbound line where she had been standing, onto the southbound line to take her back to Liverpool. Due to a signalling error, this did not happen, and the train started her journey back to Liverpool whilst still travelling on the northbound line upon which she had arrived.

Having left the station on the wrong track, the train slowly gathered speed and was travelling at about 12mph as it approached Brickfield railway sidings, located about 200 yards from the Burscough station. The locomotive hauling the train was being driven by Thomas Looney, aged 50 and his fireman, 20-year-old Robert Clarkson.

As the train was passing Brickfield sidings, a northbound express passenger train which was travelling at about 40-50mph in the opposite direction, but on the same track, ploughed head on into local train. The express train travelling north, was the 5.30pm Liverpool to Fleetwood express passenger boat-train, conveying passengers to Fleetwood to catch the ferry to Belfast in Northern Ireland. The express, which was being driven by driver John Bullfield, assisted by fireman Sam Meadows was not scheduled to stop at Burscough station, hence its speed at the time of the collision.

When the impact occurred, the express train telescoped the local train causing its driver and fireman to be killed instantly. The train guard, Edward Sutton who was travelling in the front passenger guard's compartment of the train was also killed instantly. The remaining fatal and seriously injured casualties were all passengers on board the local train travelling to Liverpool.

Mr Sawyer, the Station Master at Burscough Junction was quickly on the scene to take charge of all railway matters. He organised a special train to convey casualties to Preston for hospital treatment and two further special trains, for those passengers from both trains involved in the accident, who were fit enough to travel, to be conveyed to their destinations.

Enquiries into the accident initially focussed upon Burscough junction signal box. It transpired that signalman John Spencer had worked a day shift in the signal box and was due to finish duty at 6pm, some five minutes before the local train was due to depart for Liverpool. He later gave evidence that Anthony Meli who was working the night shift should have relieved him just before six o'clock to enable him to book off duty and go home. However, Meli was a few minutes late and entered the signal box 6.03pm. As a result of this, Spencer had already set both the signal and points (to divert the train onto the southbound track), so that the local train could depart on time at 6.05pm.

Meli later gave evidence that when he normally started work on the night shift (6pm), his first job was to set the signals and points for the departure of the 6.05pm train and the passing of the Liverpool to Fleetwood express boat train some ten minutes later. On this occasion, due to being a few minutes late, Signalman Spencer had already carried out the tasks but he himself checked to make sure that both the points and signals had been set correctly. As far as he was concerned, everything was fine.

It was only after the 6.05pm train left the station platform and started to pass the signal box that he (Meli) noticed that the train was travelling south towards Liverpool, but still on the northbound track, driving into the path of the Fleetwood express. He further stated that he grabbed a red signal lamp and waved it at the driver of the local train, by which time the engine had already passed the signal box and the driver obviously had not seen it. After that, nothing could be done to prevent the accident which occurred.

Major General Hutchinson RE, a Board of Trade Inspector, later headed an enquiry which concluded that the accident was due to a signalling error by signalman Anthony Meli and the enquiry recommended that he be indicted on charges of manslaughter in respect of all the individuals killed in the train crash.

A police investigation concluded that whilst it was possible that either signalman Meli or signalman Spencer could have accidentally set the points which caused the local train to travel on the wrong track, it was likely that Meli, whilst in a state of fluster at being slightly late for work, changed the points as he normally did, not realising that Spencer had already done so. If that was the case, changing the points again would have caused the local train to remain on the northbound track as she travelled south and the accident was inevitable. The main factor however in determining responsibility for the accident was that when the accident occurred, Meli was officially in charge of the signal box (Spencer having booked off duty), so he was fully accountable for the accident and should be indicted for manslaughter.

After a full coroner's inquest, a coroner's jury also delivered a guilty verdict against Meli and he was indicted by the coroner to stand trial on charges of manslaughter.

On Thursday, 12 February 1880, Anthony Meli, aged 27, appeared before Judge Lord Coleridge at Liverpool Assize Court charged with nine counts of manslaughter. His lordship told the jury that he had read all the depositions in this case in great detail and after careful consideration of all the evidence he could see no element of criminal negligence on the part of the defendant. He instructed the jury to return a verdict of not guilty and the case against Meli was dismissed. No further criminal charges were preferred against any other person.

On Wednesday, 11 August 1880, at a half-yearly meeting of the Lancashire and Yorkshire Railway Company held at Manchester, Thomas Barnes the Chairman of the company announced that the large sum of £12,940 (£1.6 million today) which had naturally been expected, had been paid in compensation to the unfortunate passengers killed and injured in the unfortunate accident at Burscough. He further stated that he was glad to be able to say that steps had been taken which would prevent the possibility of such an accident in the future.

Chapter 8

Other Offences

Set Fire to a Sawmill After Losing His Job

In the winter of 1867, William Richard Skeels, aged 20, was living and working at the Midland Railway Hotel Derby where he was employed as a sculleryman (kitchen worker). On Friday, 20 December, Skeels was dismissed from his job at the hotel after being found guilty of misconduct. Mr Plock, the hotel manager allowed Skeels to sleep at the hotel that evening, informing him that he must vacate his room and leave the hotel premises the following morning.

At about 2.30am on the Saturday, Skeels sneaked from his room and left the hotel by climbing through a window which he opened to avoid being seen by the night porter who was on duty at the hotel entrance. After leaving the hotel, Skeels walked across the station yard and broke into a large wooden shed-like building which was in fact the railway carriage and wagon department sawmill. Having gained access to the sawmill, Skeels took a bundle of old rags and soaked them in grease. He then proceeded to make a bonfire, using rugs, timber and other items over which he poured turpentine before igniting it.

The fire spread rapidly, engulfing the whole building which burned to the ground. Thousands of pounds worth of machinery and a large quantity of timber and other items were destroyed in the blaze. Skeels made good his escape and returned unnoticed to his hotel bedroom through the window which he had left open when leaving the hotel earlier.

Later that morning, Skeels packed his belongings and vacated the hotel as instructed by Mr Plock the previous day. After leaving the hotel, William Skeels caught a train to London where he spent several nights sleeping rough amongst the homeless.

On 31 December, at about 1am, Skeels approached Police Constable George Hulatt of the Metropolitan Police, who was performing duty in uniform in Edgware Road, West London. Skeels said to PC Hulatt, 'If you like, you can take me into custody, as I am the man who set fire to the saw mills at Derby at three o'clock in the morning.' Constable Hulatt asked, 'Why did you do that?' Skeels replied, 'Because I was dismissed from the hotel where I was working. I went across the yard and set fire to the shed. It was wilful and malicious. I was quite sober and I would do it again.'

Skeels was subsequently arrested and taken to Molyneux Police Station, Marylebone where he made a voluntary statement which he wrote himself, in the presence of Police Sergeant Radford. He admitted burning down the railway sawmill as an act of revenge against the Midland Railway Company after losing his job at the railway hotel, although he did say that it was his own fault that he lost his job and he deserved it. He further stated that he had considered burning down the Midland Hotel itself but decided not to do that because he was fond of the managers who lived and worked there, so he set fire to the sawmill at the railway station instead.

Skeels later appeared before Marlborough Street Magistrates Court in London where he was committed to stand trial for arson, before the Derbyshire Spring Assizes in March 1867. He was remanded in custody and later escorted to Derby to stand trial.

On Friday, 6 March 1868, Skeels appeared before Mr Justice Hannan at the Derbyshire Spring Assizes where he pleaded guilty to destroying the saw mill by arson. He was sentenced to seven years penal servitude.

Pub Landlord Annoyed Passengers

On Monday, 2 July 1877, James Williams, landlord of the Brunswick Hotel, Thomas Street, Sheffield caught the 5pm train from Rotherham to Sheffield. During the journey, he used bad language and insulted several passengers. When approached by the train guard, he used foul language and tore up his ticket.

Williams subsequently appeared before Sheffield Magistrates Court, charged with annoying passengers, an offence under the Manchester, Sheffield and Lincolnshire Railway byelaws. He was fined 50 shillings (£300 today), plus court costs or two months' imprisonment. He elected to pay the fine.

Guard Loses His Train

On Thursday, 30 March 1893, Martin Leonard, a carter from Bradford went to Shipley railway station to catch a train to Leeds. As he approached the station, he saw the 10.55am Bradford to Leeds passenger train standing at the station platform waiting to depart.

In fear of missing the train, instead of using the footbridge, Leonard took a short cut by running across two sets of running rails of the main line and jumping onto the platform as the Leeds train started to pull out of the station. Leonard ran after the train which was moving very slowly and caught up with the guard's van at the back of the train, just as the guard was about to step onto the running board of his guard's van to board his train.

Leonard pushed the guard to one side and jumped onto the running board of the guard's van himself. He tried three or four times to get into the guard's van but slipped on each occasion. He did however manage to hold on to the door handle of the guard's van until he eventually managed to board the train. In the meantime, the guard who Leonard had pushed aside and prevented from boarding his train and was left standing bewildered and embarrassed on the station platform as he watched his train leave the station without him.

Leeds station was swiftly informed of the incident and the train was met upon arrival some fifteen minutes later when Leonard was interviewed by railway police officers. He subsequently appeared before magistrates charged with boarding a train in motion, contrary to the railway byelaws. He pleaded not guilty but was found guilty and fined ten shillings (£67 today) plus costs or ten days' imprisonment. He elected to pay the fine.

A Duel Between Locomotives

On Saturday, 19 August 1899, Edward John Hopkins was the driver in charge of works locomotive number nine at the Cyfarthfa Steelworks, Merthyr Tyfil in South Wales. During his shift, he stopped his engine in some railway sidings in order to take on coal from a coal wagon which was stabled there specifically for the use of drivers to replenish coal in their locomotives.

While Driver Hopkins was in the process of shovelling coal into the bunker of his locomotive, another engine pulled up and stopped in front of his engine. Both engines were facing each other, bumper to bumper. This second engine was works locomotive number 10 being driven by a 23-year-old driver, William Edwards. Edwards sounded the whistle on his engine to attract the attention of driver Hopkins who was still busy shovelling coal.

Driver Hopkins looked towards Edwards who shouted at him to move his engine back a few yards as he was blocking a set of points which Edwards needed to cross in order to get to the water tower to take on some water. Hopkins ignored Edwards and carried on shovelling coal. Edwards got down from his engine, approached Hopkins and again asked him to move his locomotive as his engine was getting dangerously low on water. Hopkins told Edwards to go to hell.

Edwards then got back onto his engine (number 10), drove it forward and began to push engine number 9 backwards to clear the set of points. Hopkins ran back, jumped into the cab of his engine and retaliated by pushing engine number 10 backwards. A duel then ensued between the two locomotives, each pushing the other backwards and forward on several occasions until the buffers of both engines got jammed together and locomotive number 9 came off the track.

There was no serious damage to either locomotive but had either locomotive turned over, serious or even fatal injuries could have resulted to either of the drivers or their firemen.

After a full investigation into the matter, it was decided that driver Hopkins should not have blocked the set of points in order to take on coal and having done so, he should have moved his engine when asked, to allow driver Edwards access to the water tower as his engine was dangerously low on water.

Hopkins subsequently appeared before Merthyr Magistrates Court on 25 August 1899, charged with an offence of endangering the safety of persons upon the railway, contrary to the Offences against the Persons Act 1861, section 34. He was committed to stand trial at the Glamorgan Assizes.

Edward John Hopkins appeared before Judge Gwilym Williams at the Glamorgan Winter Assizes, held in Cardiff in November 1899. Judge Williams addressed the jury and advised that they give very serious consideration to this case. It might be that they would find that this case only arose because two engine drivers had been quarrelling and that there had been no significant damage to either locomotive and no realistic possibility of either driver being injured by the pushing of each other's engines. The jury subsequently ignored the bill of indictment and Hopkins was acquitted. In essence the jury found no case to answer.

Runaway Horse on Railway Line

At about 8am on Saturday, 1 November 1879, a man took his horse into a blacksmith's shop which was situated alongside the railway at Cheam in Surrey. The horse did not have a saddle or bridle and the owner was sitting bare-back on the animal in his shirt sleeves whilst it was being shod by the farrier. Suddenly, without warning the horse bolted out of the shop and jumped over a wall onto the railway track. The owner of the horse was petrified and clung onto it in fear of his life. The horse then ran along the track for over a mile before coming into view of Sutton railway station.

Passengers awaiting the 8.39am up-train to London Victoria stared in amazement as they watched a man in shirt sleeves riding a horse without a saddle or bridle dashing along the down main line between the metals towards the station. A train was standing in the station on the down line waiting to depart and the horse was heading straight towards it completely out of the rider's control.

As the horse was about to collide headlong into the locomotive, passengers on the Up platform gasped as the horse suddenly swerved onto the Up-line and galloped right through the station in the direction of Carshalton. As the horse and rider reached the end of the station platform, the 8.39am train came into view travelling on the Up-line directly towards the horse and rider. The animal did not slacken speed but instead, headed directly towards the advancing train.

To the horror of the passengers standing on Sutton station, a head on collision between the horse and the oncoming train appeared inevitable when suddenly, the man on horseback, with remarkable courage and presence of mind, threw himself from the horse and landed in the six-foot (the space in between the Up-line and the Down-line), narrowly escaping being struck by the oncoming train. The horse, also by a timely effort swerved and avoided being struck by the oncoming locomotive with just inches to spare and escaped after a terrifying two mile ordeal. Miraculously, the owner of the horse picked himself up and walked from the railway line, having escaped with just a few bruises.

No criminal proceedings were ever instituted in this case. Although a number of railway offences had been committed, it was no doubt considered that the offender in this case was also a victim who had already suffered enough and who was fortunate enough to have escaped without serious injury or even loss of life.

No Rabbit Pie for Sunday Lunch

On Monday, 11 August 1890, Albert Woodhead and John Bull, from Leighton Buzzard, both employed as labourers, appeared before Linslade Petty Sessions at Leighton Buzzard charged with unlawfully and wilfully trespassing upon the London and North-Western Railway on 24 May 1890, in such a manner as to expose themselves to danger.

John Hopkins, a local farmer, gave evidence that he saw the defendants running up and down the main railway line. He approached them, asked them what they were doing to which they replied, 'Looking for Sunday dinner.'

The men were in fact searching for rabbits on the railway embankment. Thomas Daverell a farmer from Chelmscote, gave corroborative evidence. Mr Walters a solicitor from London, prosecuting on behalf of the London and North Western Railway Company told the court that poaching on the railway and on farm land adjoining the area had become such a great nuisance around Leighton Buzzard that summonses had been taken out in this and other similar cases with a view to putting a stop to it.

John Bull, who had previous convictions for similar offences was fined £1 (£135 today) and ordered to pay 18s 6d costs (£125 today). Albert Woodhead who had no previous convictions was fined 1s 6d (£10 today) and 18s 6d costs. Both were given an alternative to serve fourteen days imprisonment.

Stray Animal Causes a Fatal Accident

On Tuesday, 9 September 1873, the 12.20pm express passenger train from Portsmouth to London Waterloo was travelling at speed on the London and South Western Railway main line between Godalming and Guildford when the driver encountered a bullock walking towards him on the railway line.

The driver immediately shut off steam and applied the brakes of the locomotive but the train was unable to stop in time to avoid a collision. The locomotive drove headlong into the animal whilst travelling at about 35mph, killing it instantly. The force of the impact was such that the locomotive was derailed and ten carriages were thrown down a steep railway embankment into a field below. The driver and fireman jumped from their locomotive before impact and survived the accident with minor injuries.

However, a number of passengers on the train were not so lucky. Two female passengers and a young boy were killed in the accident and at least thirty injured, some of them seriously. It was later established that the accident was caused by someone omitting to fasten a level crossing gate after using it in order to cross over the railway. This enabled the animal to wander onto the railway line and cause this tragic accident.

Colonel Hutchinson was later appointed to carry out a Board of Trade enquiry into the accident and his report was later published which suggested that consideration should be given to have locomotives fitted with some sort of appliance at the front of the engine for throwing off the line any obstructions which may be encountered, similar to the cow catchers invented in 1838 by British engineer Charles Babbage and extensively used in North America and other countries at the time. It was subsequently decided that such devices were not necessary on the railways in Britain.

Omitting to fasten a railway crossing gate was and still is a criminal offence by virtue of the Railway Clauses Consolidation Act of 1845 and although all railway level crossing gates which are opened manually have warning signs for the benefit of users, many people often fail to realise the dangers of leaving open such gates after use. In serious cases such as this one, any person omitting to fasten a railway crossing gate after use, which is in itself an unlawful act, is also liable to be charged with a much more serious offence of endangering the life or safety of passengers or persons upon the railway.

The person responsible for causing this particular accident by omitted to fasten the crossing gate after use was never apprehended, but the case clearly outlines the dangers involved the use of un-manned railway crossings and the reason why laws and regulations such as 'omitting to fasten gates' were introduced to govern and control their use as well as ensuring the safety of passengers and other people on the railway.

Steam Locomotives Prohibited from Emitting Smoke

Very few people are aware that in the early years of railway development, steam locomotives were prohibited from emitting smoke. Steam engines were expected to burn smokeless fuel (coke) or if using fuel which did emit smoke such as coal or wood, the locomotives had to be constructed in such a manner as to consume their own smoke.

This was one of the conditions imposed on the owners of early steam locomotives such as the *Rocket,* and the other locomotives which took part in the Rainhill Trials on the Liverpool and Manchester Railway in 1829. The matter was subsequently followed up by parliamentary legislation introduced in 1845 which made it a criminal offence for railway companies and other users of steam locomotives on a railway to allow them to emit smoke into the atmosphere. Believe it or not, environmentalists are not people who suddenly appeared in Britain during the twentieth or twenty-first centuries. A few active environmentalists were around back in the day when the railways were being constructed and Queen Victoria sat on the throne.

A number of railway companies were successfully prosecuted and fined during the nineteenth century for using locomotives which emitted smoke. Outlined below is an example of one particular railway company which fell foul of the law in this respect.

On Tuesday, 22 September 1857, the Manchester, Sheffield and Lincolnshire Railway Company were fined the sum of £5 by magistrates sitting at Sheffield Town Hall, for allowing one of their locomotives (number 77) to emit dense black smoke for seventeen minutes whilst standing on the railway line near Sheffield Goods Station. Action against the railway company was brought by Mr Cash, a consulting smoke inspector from Sheffield, for a breach of section 114 of the Railway Clauses Consolidation Act of 1845, which stated that every locomotive steam engine to be used on the railway shall, if it uses coal or other similar fuel emitting smoke, be constructed on the principle of consuming its own smoke. If any engine is not so constructed, the company or party using such engine shall forfeit five pounds for every day during which such engine shall be used on the railway (£5 in 1845 is equivalent to almost £650 today).

The railway company pleaded not guilty to the charge and was represented by Mr Styles, a solicitor employed by the company itself. Mr Styles informed magistrates that locomotive number 77, like all other locomotives owned by the company, was constructed with a view to the consuming its own smoke but it was very difficult to burn coal and prevent the emission of smoke entirely. Locomotives did emit smoke occasionally when they were standing and to substitute coal for coke was not a viable option as it would seriously increase the company's working expenses.

Mr Bailey (prosecutor) told magistrates that dense smoke was often emitted by locomotives, which not only caused serious annoyance to residents in adjacent streets, but also caused injury to health and vegetation. He went on to say that he did not see how the railway company could avoid a conviction, unless they could prove that no smoke was emitted from their locomotives. He also stated that there was no power of mitigation on behalf of the company in these cases.

The company was subsequently found guilty and fined £5. It would appear that the magistrates were satisfied that the locomotives being used by the Manchester, Sheffield and Lincolnshire Railway Company were constructed with a view to consuming their own smoke as they stopped short of imposing further fines on the company for each subsequent day that locomotive number 77 remained operational.

Prosecutions, albeit not in any great numbers, continued to be brought against individual railway companies in respect of smoke emissions throughout the Victorian era, usually by or on behalf of local authorities and as late as 1897, the London and North Western Railway Company were subject to proceedings at Stockport Magistrates Court where they were fined even though the court heard that the locomotive concerned was fitted with the latest appliance for the prevention of smoke which was working perfectly at the time. The chairman of the bench stated that the action had been brought against the railway company in the public interest.

In July 1905, a case was heard at Worship Street magistrate's court in London after being instigated by the London County Council against the Great Eastern Railway Company. It was alleged that GER locomotive number 363 had emitted black smoke whilst operating on the East London railway line. Although it was accepted that some smoke was emitted by the locomotive, the magistrate decided in favour of the railway company by dismissing the case on the grounds that a Regulation of Railways Act passed in 1868 had amended section 114 of the Railway Clauses Consolidation Act of Act of 1845, inasmuch as locomotives were only required to consume their own smoke 'as far as practicable'. This implied that an engine was not prohibited from discharging any smoke whatsoever. The full judgment as outlined in detail by Metropolitan Police Magistrate Albert Roland Cluer who heard the case, was published in the *Railway News* journal on 25 November 1905.

Although this judgment was made in a magistrate's court and had no legal precedent in law, it does appear to have had a profound effect in cases of this nature as no further prosecutions were ever instigated against a railway company for allowing a steam locomotive to discharge smoke. Although locomotives were built with a view to consuming some of their own smoke and soot deposits, locomotives often produced large quantities of smoke as they increased in size and particularly after the Second World War when many locomotives were burning poor quality coal.

In modern times, the effects of greenhouse gases are well known and public awareness of the dangers involving air pollution is at an all-time high. During the nineteenth and twentieth centuries, however, when the nation was fuelled by coal, public attitudes were somewhat different. Society in general welcomed new industrial techniques and innovations and the mass production of goods were embraced by the public at large. Steam locomotives replaced horses as the main mode of transport and by the latter part of the nineteenth century, people were captivated by the speed at which they could travel and the plumes of smoke being discharged through the chimneys of these magnificent new and shiny machines made them, stylish, lifelike and exciting which enthralled many children and adults alike.

When almost every household in the country had a coal fire, pollution was accepted as a part of everyday life and sayings such as 'don't be afraid to get your hands dirty' and 'where there's muck there's money' were familiar phrases used by the working classes. It was generally accepted that tolerating the soot, dirt and grime created during the nineteenth century and the introduction of steam locomotives and other sources of power by burning of fossil fuels far outweighed the adverse effects of smoke emissions and other forms of pollution. This of course was and still is a matter of opinion.

In practice however, it was never realistic to expect steam locomotives to operate effectively without emitting smoke and although legislation was introduced in the 1840s to prevent locomotives from doing so, the offence created was little more than a token gesture to appease certain sections of society and infringements of the legislation by railway companies was for the most part ignored. The actual numbers of prosecutions instigated against railway companies for allowing their locomotives to emit smoke was miniscule compared with the many thousands of locomotives in daily use. On the other hand, had the offence been rigorously enforced, Britain's railway network would quickly have ground to a halt. Fortunately, that did not occur.

About the Author

Afterleaving school, Malcolm Clegg enjoyed a thirty-year career with the British Transport Police. He served both in uniform and in CID, working mainly in South Wales, policing the railway network. He did, however, work for a number of years as a Docks Constable at Cardiff and Newport Docks and later worked for several years as a Uniform Sergeant at Swansea and Port Talbot Docks. In addition, almost a decade of his career was spent working at various locations in London.

The final ten years of his service were spent as a Detective Sergeant based in Swansea, investigating crimes committed on the Docks and Railway premises over an extensive area of South and West Wales which included Fishguard Harbour, incorporating the then Sealink passenger ferry services which operated between Fishguard and Rosslare in Ireland.

After his retirement, he became an active member of the British Transport Police History Group (www.btphg.org.uk). He has carried out extensive research on behalf of the group and has written a number of articles. He has written four other books: *British Steam Locomotives before Preservation; The Last Days of British Steam; LMS and LNER Steam Locomotives;* and *British Transport Police (A definitive history of the early years and subsequent development)*, each published by Pen & Sword.

He has lived in Swansea, South Wales for the past 45 years.

Index